THE FLIGHT OF WINGED WOLF

Heather Hughes-Calero

Cover Painting by Charles Frizzell
Illustrations by Diane Forney

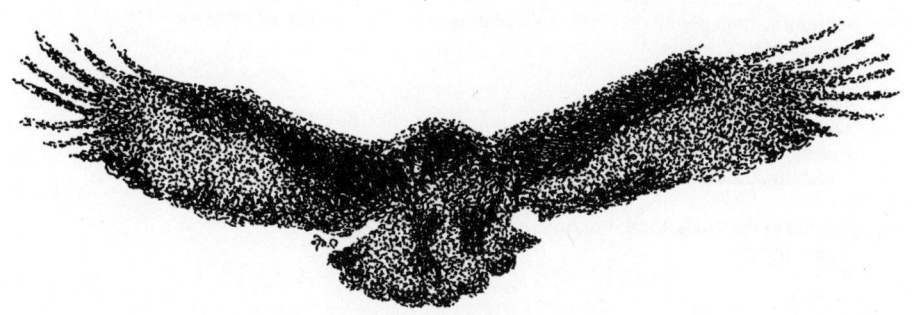

Higher Consciousness Books
1991

This is a true experience; however, the names of places, persons and facts may have been altered to protect the privacy of those involved.

Cover from the original painting "Wa Wakan Wi"
by Charles Frizzell, © Frizzell Studios, 1990.
Illustrations by Diane Forney

Higher Consciousness Books
Division of Coastline Publishing Company, Post Office Box 223062, Carmel, California 93922. Shipping and orders should be addressed to Post Office Box 299, Vineburg, California 95487. (707) 935-7012.

Printed in the United States of America
First Edition

Library of Congress Catalog No.: 91-073187
ISBN: 0-932927-08-4

To my mother Vi Maticic
with love and appreciation
for her friendship and moral support.

As she flies on
    looking at the earth with
        super-eyed focus

She sees movement,
    an energy story
      creating winds of its own
        to earful listeners

She enters the world with a glance.
    She knows she sees all without
      disturbing the illusion of
        fears and safety
          As she flies on

—ALANA

TABLE OF CONTENTS

CHAPTER 1   7
Multiple Identities

CHAPTER 2   21
Aligning Companion Energies

CHAPTER 3   33
Receiving a Power Name

CHAPTER 4   45
Learning About 'Matching Energies'

CHAPTER 5   59
Decision Making

CHAPTER 6   71
Developing Mental Power

CHAPTER 7   83
More About Companion Energy

CHAPTER 8   93
Setting Things Right

CHAPTER 9   107
The Truth About Higher Consciousness

CHAPTER 10   121
Experiences with the Animals

CHAPTER 11   131
Living as a Spiritual Warrior

CHAPTER 12   143
Flight of Winged Wolf

CHAPTER 1
MULTIPLE IDENTITIES

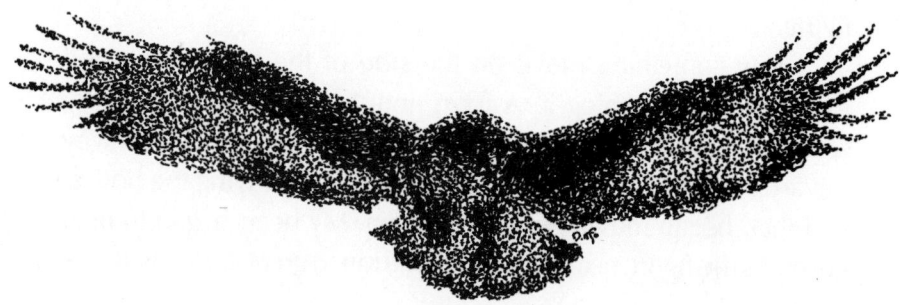

I drew in a deep breath and shivered as I stood on the front porch and looked up to the mountains. It was an extraordinary mid-summer Colorado night, barely lit by the sliver of a new moon. The stars sparkled and winked, and occasionally one fell in a perfect silver streak across the clear, dark sky. The air stirred around me, the slight trickle of a breeze was super-scented with sage and pine, exaggerated by high altitude and the left-over warmth of the day. I was excited to be back. It had been a half a year since I had left the ranch and I had forgotten the intensity of 8800 foot altitude; how there was unusual clarity to the forms of things even in darkness, and how the clarity seemed to heighten one's awareness about what there was to be seen, as well as what was unseen.

The trail that led up behind the mountain into the hollow was barely visible and I presumed that I would have to wait until the following day to see Alana. I wondered what it would be like to be in her presence again after months of separation. Would she be happy to see me, or angry that I had come? While it was my ranch, I had accepted her as my teacher and she had told me to busy myself in the world, lecturing and conducting seminars on the meaning of Shamanism, demystifying it for people so that they could apply the spiritual principles as useful everyday tools for living.

I saw something move on the side of the hill and I stood motionlessly, watching it. A form, indistinguishable at first, descended the trail that led from the hollow and slowly made its way toward me. For a brief instant it paused, as if studying the house, and then began moving toward it again. My heart began to beat faster. As the figure neared, a part of me ran to greet it. I knew it was Alana.

She approached the house and stood below the porch, looking up at me. Even though I could not clearly see her face, I recognized the blue coveralls and the slope of the shoulders that held them up. I thought she was smiling.

I called to her excitedly. "Hello, Alana."

She straightened her body and seemed to examine me. It was as though I could feel her deep-set, dark blue eyes upon me.

"Hello, Heather," she answered back. "Where did you come from?"

I was surprised that she was surprised to see me. For weeks prior to my coming I had felt drawn to return, as if she was inwardly calling me. "I drove in from California," I answered uneasily.

"So I see," she said eyeing me.

"I had the feeling that you wanted me to come," I explained, "that you felt I had been away too long."

She chuckled to herself, then said, "More like the feeling that you wanted me to want you to come so you could show me something."

I was astounded and did not answer. While I had come because I had felt drawn to return, I had come to show her our book.

She climbed the porch steps and stood looking at me and then smiled as though she had suddenly decided that she was pleased to see me. "What is it that you want me to see?" she asked.

I forced my eyes from hers and hurried inside to the book on top of my handbag and turned to give it to her as she walked through the door. It was a copy of *Woman Between the Wind.*

She looked at it, turned it over in her hands as if feeling the contents through the covers, and then opened it. The first page that she saw contained her poem "The Shape Shifter." Her eyes settled on the page, and she began to slowly speak the words aloud.

> *Listen!*
> > *The wind calls me from my left.*
>
> *I look out my window. The snow*
> *speaks to me of stories found on the*
> *surface of the breathing earth.*
>
> > *The snow parts, the earth*
> > *breathes, the sun shines.*
> > *The trees stand naked with*
> > *branches defining the wind.*
> > *The wind appears speaking of energy,*
> > *through visionary maps the branches*
> > *define on the surface of infinity.*
> *My heart.*
> > *My quiet heart*
> > > *returns with stories.*

Now—My heart beats;
the wind is no longer invisible.
My fear. My fear
of her power, her sound,
her presence. My fear is now
lessened.

She is my breath, my aloneness, my
joy, my uneasiness. She is around me.
She goes inside & outside of me.
She is everywhere.

I am transcending.

I have become the current in the sky.

I am between her. She is between
me. Both reaching for the other side.
Both kissing what we are not,
Always trapped on the
otherside.

We fight to get out.
We fight to get in.

We meet each other after the fight -
In the calm
In the land
In between.

She looked at me and gazed into my my eyes. "I guess you're ready," she said.

I wanted to ask, "Ready for what?" but I waited for her to go on.

"What time is it?" she asked.

I lowered my eyes to glance at my watch. "Ten past ten."

"Drive me to town," she said.

"Eastcliffe?" The idea did not appeal to me at all. It was a forty-five minute drive into town and I was exhausted from my two-day journey from California.

"Yes," she said, hesitantly, noting my resistance. "I can't tell you why now, but you will understand when we get there." She placed the book on the burlwood coffee table in front of the couch and started for the door.

I started to object, to ask her to please wait until the morning, but inwardly I reminded myself that it was not my position to complain. It was then that I heard a little voice inside of myself explain, "She is trying to wear you down so that she can get a better grip on your spirit. If you want to work with Alana, you do it her way."

"It's important that we go now," Alana said as if listening to my thought. She went out the door and headed for the Jeep.

It occurred to me that the gas stations were closed and that if we went we might not have enough gas to get back. I ran after her and explained. She glared at me as though I had plotted an excuse and then got into the Jeep. I grabbed my handbag and went after her.

Fatigue agitated me and set me dumbly fuming over the fact that she felt that wherever she wanted to go was more important than my rest, but I gradually caught hold of myself. We drove silently until we came to the edge of town where I applied the brakes in the dark street in a "what do I do now" manner. There was one street light at the far end of the main street. All the rest of the town was dark. I couldn't see my watch but I knew it must be near eleven.

"Go on to Smith's Theater," Alana said in a quiet voice.

I released the brakes and allowed the car to roll down the street to the street light in front of Smith's Theater. I pulled in next to it and cut the motor. The theater was boarded up and had been for the past three years that it had been out of operation.

Alana got out of the car and then motioned me to follow. She walked past the front of the theater to the side entrance where she slid a key into the lock on the heavy metal exit door and opened it, going inside. I was surprised but said nothing and followed her. She flipped a switch as we entered.

The theatre was lit by the faint glow of aisle lights at the foot of the rows, just enough light to show me that we had entered by the first row, beneath the stage. I hesitated to gaze into the semi-darkness as if expecting to see someone.

"There's no one here but us, " Alana said, reassurringly, as if she knew my concern. She made her way to the center of the first row and sat down. "I'll sit here. You go up onto the stage."

I remained where I was, standing at the end of the aisle, looking up at the semi-dark stage. I was somewhat frightened by the absurdity of her request, as well as still angry at having to drive into town, and I was sure that Alana knew what I was feeling.

"Well, go on," she prodded.

"But Alana..." I caught the protest before it escaped my lips. I still had control enough to remind myself that I had promised never to argue with her again.

"The stairs are over there." She pointed to the far end of the stage.

I was reluctant, but went to the stairs as I had been told, and climbed them to step up upon the stage.

"Go to the center." She waved me over with her hand.

I walked to the center and looked down at Alana sitting just beneath me.

"Don't look at me! Look at the audience."

"But there is no one here."

"Pretend! Heather, you're a writer. You know how to do it."

I wasn't sure what she wanted of me. I wished we had stayed at the ranch, sat and talked awhile to catch up on the past six months before she tried to teach me something new. She had given us no time to get reacquainted, not that I should have been surprised. There had never been anything about Alana that had met my expectations. It was foolish of me to expect our reunion to be anything different. From our very first meeting, I realized that she was unlike anyone I had ever known. It wasn't long after that I came to recognize her power as a medicine woman and how devastating it felt to resist her. I don't know why I expected to meet her as a friend and peer now. She was still my teacher.

"Bang, bang, bang, bang." It took me a moment to realize that Alana was stomping her feet on the cement floor beneath her seat, like someone impatient for the movie to begin.

I was uncertain what she wanted me to do.

"This is the day of the talkie," she yelled. "Talk about something. Tell me what you're doing!"

"I'm not doing anything, Alana," I whined, feeling totally out of sorts, "and I don't know what to say. I don't know what you want me to do. I don't know why we came or what you expect of me, or what I'm supposed to expect of you for that matter." I hesitated as though I was dreaming and something unnerving was about to happen. I could feel her eyes full upon me. She began to stomp her feet on the cement floor again. I was annoyed.

"Alana, why are you making me stand up here like a fool on a stage? I'm your student. I give you my love, my devotion, and you treat me like I'm an idiot." I stared at her for a long moment, my arms reaching out dramatically in front of me.

"Bravo, bravo!" Alana yelled, while stomping her feet on the cement.

I looked at her, too astonished to speak.

"Yes, indeed! That was a fine piece of acting...but I didn't like the plot too much."

"Alana, why are you taunting me?" I asked pathetically.

She shook her head. "No, I don't think I would like that one either."

I became furious. "I am not play acting!" I shot back. "I am trying to communicate to you how I feel and you treat me like a fool. I came here at great expense, and not merely financial expense. I sacrificed a great many things to be here, whether you feel that sacrifice is important or not."

"Boooo...booo!" she suddenly yelled. "If I were you I wouldn't make a play for martyrdom. You would be terrible at it. Please do something else."

I realized she was egging me on and so I changed my approach. "Believe me, Alana...I don't wish to act at anything. I wish to live a life of Doing!" I emphasized the word "do" in the way she had taught me to use it, meaning to live life, not merely talk about it.

She stood up and walked to the foot of the stage, looking up at me. "Good idea, do something."

"I don't know what you want of me, Alana."

"Anything...you say you like to do, DO something!"

I hesitated, uncertain what she wanted from me.

"Act out how one crosses the street," she called out, and then sat back down and waited.

After a moment, I turned sideways, looked both ways as if expecting to see cars coming, and then carefully proceeded straight ahead, as if I was crossing the street.

"Good," Alana called up to me. "Now go in that building over there."

The empty stage was the building but I went to the center of it and pretended to open a door and go inside. Suddenly I got caught up in the game. Instead of turning to Alana and asking for direction, I pretended to meet someone and began to talk to them about their family, finally excusing myself to catch the elevator. Once up to the top floor, I went out onto the roof, looked out over the city below and spoke my thoughts aloud.

"I feel so alone and yet I carry my teacher in my heart. I am alone, totally alone and yet I am filled with love for life, for learning, for spiritually developing, for freedom, for teaching freedom. I am the teacher and the teacher is me. I am freedom and freedom is me." Then I fell silent.

Alana quietly stood up. "Let's go back to the ranch," she said.

On the way to the ranch, Alana began to tell me about the wild horses. Stony, the lead stallion, had hurt his leg. While she had been nursing him, she said the wound was severe enough that she didn't believe he would ever be the same. She blamed herself for the accident, claiming that she had called him to her at a moment when she should have left him alone. "My timing was off," she said, "and so I am responsible."

I knew that accidents were the result of one's split attention, but I suggested that the responsibility was not her's—that Stony should take responsibility for himself.

She turned her head, glaring at me from the passenger seat. "I am a medicine woman," she said in a firm voice. "Who or whatever I call to me responds to my protection."

I nodded that I understood. It was a principle I believed in and I knew that I had made excuses for her merely to help her feel better about it.

"I don't tell you things for your approval or disapproval," Alana said. "I tell you things to educate you. Sometimes I must sacrifice myself in the process."

I didn't know what to say and so I decided to change the subject. I began to marvel at the beauty of the place, how I had almost forgotten the feeling of exhilaration that came with being in 8800 foot altitude.

"This is a beautiful place," she agreed, "but I told you before it isn't the beauty of a place that is valuable but how we perceive it."

I explained that I knew that, that I had been merely making small talk to ease the fatigue of driving so many miles in one day.

"You think I am a difficult teacher, don't you, Heather? " She paused, watching me. "You are here to work. I have a great many important things to teach you in our short time together. We will have to make the best of each moment."

A part of me wished that I had never come. It seemed that while I was away from Alana, I yearned to be with her, fantasizing how happy I felt in her presence, and it was true, but being with her was also painful. I was always changing in her presence. Being with Alana was like biting into a bittersweet chocolate bar. It made your jaw ache but it tasted good at the same time. I turned to her and nodded with a grin. I did think she was a difficult teacher, the most difficult I had ever had, or heard of, or even read about. And I didn't know that I had come so much to work, as to share the fruits of our labors. I believed I had come to refresh myself and then return to my work in the world.

"Why haven't you asked me about what we did at the movie house?" she asked.

"I knew you would tell me when it was time," I said, not really wanting to discuss it. The fatigue of my trip was catching up with me.

"It is time for you to ask me," she said.

"What did we do at the theater tonight?"

"What do you think we did?"

I was too tired to think. "I don't know, Alana. That's why I asked you."

She let out a sigh, which made me wish I had forced a better answer.

"I was a player on a stage," I added quickly.

"Good. Tell me more."

"In life, we are like players on a stage. Each of us is a featured player, a character actor with many personalities and many roles inside of us."

Alana smiled. "Yes, and you have hit on my reason for having you perform."

I waited, turning my head slowly back and forth from the road to Alana, soaking in the unusual demeanor of the medicine woman. She was an Indian with dark blue eyes and at least a hundred different faces. From moment to moment she seemed to change. She was both old and young, round-faced and slim, kind and cruel. I was never really certain which one of her I would be talking to.

"Stop the car!" she said.

I brought the car to a quick halt and turned to her. She looked me kindly in the eyes. "It is my responsibility to show you your schizophrenia," she said softly.

Her unusually gentle manner added to the nature of her words and I felt suddenly alert and awake. I turned away and put the Jeep in gear and began to drive down the road again. I wondered if she had heard what I had been thinking? Did she believe me to be as unusual as I believed her to be?

"Heather, you are schizophrenic!"

The Jeep swerved as the shock of her words penetrated me. It was as if I had been plunged into a bad dream. What did she mean? It seemed to me that if either of us were schizophrenic, it was her. I recalled countless times when her face seemed to change before my eyes. She seemed old one moment, middle-aged or young the next. Sometimes she appeared to be two entirely different persons, and I had often thought that if I had had photographs of her at various times, it would prove that she was many different people in one body.

"Do you know what schizophrenia means?" she asked.

"To have a multiple or split personality."

"Yes, and no. That is the answer that society gives but they have little understanding of what it means. If they did, they wouldn't give such a simplistic answer. Let me ask you this. Do you know what causes the condition?

"Schizophrenia occurs when an individual is in conflict between their thoughts and their emotions. They think one thing and feel the opposite, like you." She paused, studying my uneasy expression. "You say to yourself that you think thus and so and then you feel you shouldn't have thought that and so your feelings are always in conflict with what you're thinking." She stared at me, waiting for some kind of response. Finally, I nodded that I understood. "Don't feel put off by what I am telling you, Heather. You're not alone. Most people are schizophrenic."

I didn't react, instead I waited for her to go on.

"You're better now than when I met you," Alana continued. "In the early days I couldn't have said to you that you were schizophrenic without having you fly into a rage, or at best argue with me. But, nevertheless, the condition still exists in you. Can you sense it?"

While Alana was talking I had been thinking that what she was saying was true and, at the same time, I recognized that I was inwardly arguing that what she was saying had nothing to do with me.

"Schizophrenics live in a fantasy world most of the time," Alana went on. "They hallucinate experiences and delude themselves into believing that certain conditions in their life are true when they aren't. Then, because of the circumstances they've set up for themselves, they become increasingly passive and indifferent to the environment."

In some ways I could understand and relate to what Alana was saying. I knew that very often I lived in my own world; however, because of my work, I was becoming more and more aware of the world outside of my own. I was no longer passive or indifferent, and I told her so.

Alana smiled and looked deeply into me. "Your progress pleases me, Heather. I actually think you will become a medicine woman, after all." She paused, gazing at me. "When I first met you, I had my doubts. Oh, you managed well enough in the world, and like most people, you seemed normal, but your disorder held you back in life just the same. You could never quite push through the barriers in your life because you deluded yourself in believing that the barriers were your life." She paused again, chuckling to herself. "Do you remember the keychain I saw back in Colorado in Swedes Feed Store that read "I brake for hallucinations?" I asked you to buy it for yourself, but you were insulted. Do you remember?"

I nodded, and remembered how embarrassed and angry I had been at the suggestion.

She sighed with relief. "You are getting well, Heather, and through your work, you will help others get well. You will show people how to fulfill themselves so that their real world will be better than any fantasy they can make for themselves. Remember, a Shaman doesn't change things in people, a Shaman fixes things."

I was still confused about the idea of multiple personalities alive in each of us and I asked her how she knew it. I also told her how her face often appeared to change when she was talking to me.

"We all have multiple personalities," she explained. "We change our minds, our feelings, and when our attitudes change our entire countenance changes with it. The difference between an ordinary schizophrenic person and a Shaman, is that the Shaman is aware of her shape shifts and the ordinary individual is not. In fact, the Shaman often uses shape shifts to heal another person or a situation. A Shaman is so adept at shape shifting that he or she can become like a river, or a drop of water, or a mountain lion, a wolf, or even an eagle." She stopped speaking. Her entire face was radiant, as if a beam of light had been turned upon her and she was smiling at me. I had never seen her look so beautiful.

"That brings us to the real reason you are here, in Colorado," Alana said, breaking the magical silence. "I was able to call you here because of your love for it. It is here in Colorado, that you will discover your power self. You will learn your true name and how to call upon it to serve in your mission in life."

My skin prickled as she talked and I knew that what she had said was about to come to pass, yet a voice within myself said, "Be careful. Do not give yourself over totally to her. Retain your center."

CHAPTER 2

ALIGNING COMPANION ENERGIES

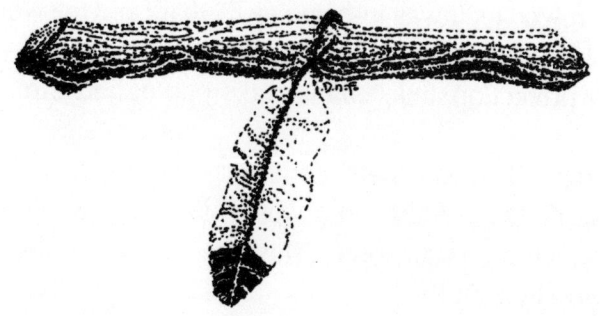

Alana was at my door ready to take me into the hills early in the morning. I had been asleep when her knock came and rushed to get dressed and gather a few supplies together. I suggested to her that we have something to eat before we leave.

"Don't worry about it," she said, "it's already waiting for us."

I asked her to explain.

"You'll find out soon enough," she said, then told me that we had to leave. She started for the door.

"Can't I take time to brush my teeth first!" I yelled, hoping she would slow down a bit.

"You can do that later."

I thought of telling her that I had spent a fortune on my teeth and that it would be wise for me to spend the first two minutes of the day attending to them, but I managed to hold my tongue. I hurried after her. When we reached the trail and I had settled down, Alana handed me a stick. Then she started up the side of the mountain and waited for me to catch up. "That stick is no ordinary stick," she said with a sideways glance.

I studied the three-foot stick she had given me, running my fingers over the patterns that were etched into it by worms that had once burrowed their way in-between the bark and the wood itself. It was a beautiful pattern, not quite like any other I had seen.

"It's a protection stick," Alana said, stopping and turning to face me.

I thought she meant that the stick was like a fetish and I said so.

"Yes, it's like a fetish, in a way," she said. "A certain fetish protects you from certain forces. This stick is a certain fetish that will protect you from Bull."

"There are bulls on the property?" I asked.

"Not bulls, but Bull. We call him Bull. He's a man...and he's angry at you."

"At me? Why me?" I asked, suddenly concerned. I had no enemies that I knew of, no one that would physically harm me, and I told her so.

"Bull is angry at you because he felt your uncle should have left him the property and not you," Alana said.

"Was he related to my uncle?"

"No, but your uncle treated him like a son. Bull was always there when he needed him, and he did most of the work around the place." Alana turned and started up the hill again. I went running after her.

"Why is it you never told me about Bull before?" I asked.

"It didn't seem to be necessary," Alana said, keeping her attention on the trail. "When your Uncle Farley died, Bull went into such a depressed state that he left town. No one had seen him until just recently, and he seems crazy with anger toward you."

"It's not my fault my uncle left me the place," I said excitedly. "I never asked for it. I didn't even know about it."

"That's just the point," Alana said. Bull thinks you should have given it to him, that you have no right to it."

"That is ridiculous," I said, determined not to feel threatened.

"No, it's not, and I would be careful if I were you," Alana said. "Bull is not quite right between the ears and your uncle knew it." She tapped the top of her head with her index finger and then whirled her finger clockwise next to her head.

"When did he get back?"

"Last week."

"Where is he now?" I asked uneasily.

Alana shrugged her shoulders. "Probably with the others," she said.

Alana had mentioned at one time that there were others living in the hills. I assumed they were Indian friends of hers and that one day she would introduce me. I asked her if it was they who she meant.

She didn't answer. At that moment she turned sideways and slipped through the passageway into the hollow.

The hollow was bathed in dew and spotlighted with early morning sunlight. It was even more beautiful than I had remembered. "Just be careful," she whispered, "and keep the stick with you."

The manner in which she whispered made me afraid to speak. I looked about the hollow but saw no one. There was not even an animal in sight. I stayed close to her side and walked in step with her. Suddenly, she stopped and stood listening.

"Alana, what do you hear?"

She didn't answer.

I looked all around us but saw nothing.

"There's someone up ahead and I was listening for a clue to who it was," she whispered.

I listened but still heard nothing but the sound of birds and told her so.

"Listen beyond the obvious sounds of nature," she instructed. "Listen for sounds treading the earth."

At first I heard nothing and was about to tell her so when I noticed a dull hum coming from the ground. I squatted to hear it better. "What is it?" I asked.

"The earth records all movement," Alana explained. "If we listen to her and learn the meaning of her sounds, we can see a person before they approach."

"Can you tell who it is?"

"It's not Bull," she said with some relief. "If it was Bull, the vibrations would be coarser, because of his anger." She looked at me when she said anger.

I refused to be intimidated. "Alana, I'm not angry at him, so I have nothing to fear."

"Always fear a person who is angry," she said. "The anger of one robs the power of another."

A chill ran up the back of my legs and settled in my lower back.

Alana pointed into the distance.

I looked to see a hawk swoop down from the cliff and land on a boulder in the center of the field. Then there was another and another.

I turned to Alana with a start, but she kept walking and

motioned me to follow her. As we approached the boulder, the hawks took to flight, circled us, flew away and then flew back again. Suddenly, as if out of nowhere, a woman came walking toward us. She was a light-skinned woman about my age and build and she wore a fringed buckskin dress adorned with feathers. Her sandy colored hair fell loose about her shoulders. Hanging from her neck in the center of her chest was a cluster of crystals. She was smiling. I thought she looked like a New Age hippie.

Alana turned to me and drew me alongside her, then she took my hand and placed it between hers and the woman's. "This is Heather."

"Hello, Heather."

I looked into the woman's kindly face. Like Alana she seemed ageless.

"My name is Terra Lenda. You may call me Terra." A hawk swooped down and momentarily suspended itself over her head.

I was both fascinated by the hovering of the hawk and the penetrating gaze of the woman's eyes and I suddenly had the odd feeling that I was dreaming. "Hello, Terra," I answered as if from afar.

Alana chuckled and lowered her hand, removing it from beneath mine. Terra Lenda removed hers as well. I lowered mine. "Heather is taken by you and she's unsure if she's awake or asleep," Alana said, making fun of what I was feeling.

Terra Lenda smiled and stepped back as if to get a different view of me. A second hawk was now hovering over her head. "I see that there is a part of her that is asleep, but that she will awaken quickly."

"I hope you're right," Alana said, talking about me as if I wasn't there. When my eyes shifted to meet hers, she burst out laughing. "Heather, don't be so serious. It is your seriousness that keeps a part of you asleep. Your seriousness would rather have you believe that you are dreaming than to admit that you are who you are in the company of other medicine women."

Alana's words enveloped me. I was struck by the impression that she had included me in her collective usage of the term "medicine women" but I knew that if I drew attention to it, she would deny that she had said it. She was teasing me, but not unkindly, and I could not help but be aware of a rare affectionate undertone and be pleased by it. I was sure, however, that her teasing was purposeful. I smiled in an effort to lighten up, but the distant feeling between myself and Alana and Terra Lenda grew more pronounced.

"Heather doesn't know?" Terra Lenda said with some surprise in her voice.

"Not yet," Alana answered. "She prefers to think that she is a lowly student in the company of her teachers and that we are better than she is...that we are above her." She paused and sucked in a deep breath of air through her teeth. "And it would have helped, Terra, if you had come as an Indian."

Terra looked at me and grinned. Having grown accustomed to Alana's sarcasm toward me, I grinned in return. While I knew Terra wasn't Indian, for an instant she appeared to be. As I studied the fine features of her face I realized that her cheekbones were high and that her eyes were dark, not blue like Alana's. I quickly turned to Alana, who was chuckling at me. "I never did tell you Heather," Alana said, "that I am Lokota, a Sioux medicine woman. Terra is..."

Before she finished her sentence, in my dazed state, I reached out and tapped her on the shoulder with the open palm of my hand. "You're trying to trick me," I said, as if I had just caught on to the joke.

Alana's expression suddenly changed, her face darkened angrily and, glaring at me, she snarled, "Heather, don't you ever strike me again!"

I was stunned and didn't know what to say.

"Did you hear me?" she shrieked.

I felt sick, as if I had opened a can of worms and was forced to eat them. "Alana, I didn't strike you," I said pathetically.

"Yes, you did! And it hurt!"

I hesitated, hoping she was going to suddenly laugh and tell me that the incident was a joke.

"If you ever strike me again, we're through. Do you understand?" she growled.

"You mean I'll be off the hook?" I teased in an effort to break the heavy feeling between us. I was sure she was mocking up her anger, that she was merely trying to get me to react.

"I can't work with you Heather," she said cooly.

"Alana, may we please stop this game."

"You really do not understand, do you Heather?"

I hesitated, feeling that she may suddenly reveal the true meaning to her words, that we would laugh and move on to something else. Perhaps it wasn't polite of me to tap her on the shoulder, but it seemed nothing to create such a fuss.

"Answer me!" she shrieked.

A hawk screeched somewhere nearby and the dream-like sensation I had been feeling intensified. I wondered if I could be back at the ranch asleep, or that our entire meeting was a dream, that I had never left California. If it was a dream, I need only continue dreaming and, sooner or later, I would awaken.

"Heather, are you deaf?"

I used my most sincere tone of voice to answer her. "Alana, I really don't know what you're talking about. I didn't strike you, I merely tapped you on the shoulder."

"You hit me and it hurt!"

I was becoming flustered at having to explain what I didn't feel needed explaining. I recalled how Alana had said that I was too serious and it occurred to me that she was using new tactics to loosen me up. I decided to let her know that I had a sense of humor and I let out a laugh.

She glared at me.

"Ha! Ha!" I laughed again. Then, after not getting a favorable response, I said, "I don't think this game is very funny."

Her eyes narrowed as she continued to glare at me, then she nodded her head as if she had just discovered something. "Heather, I've been wrong about you. I don't know how I could have been so wrong, but I have been. I can't work with you. You and I are totally different. I can't teach you because you don't even understand what I am trying to teach you." She turned away.

I was annoyed by her unfairness. "Alana, why are you picking on me?"

There was a moment of silence. "Heather, I want you to leave," she said with her back to me.

"Leave?" Certainly she couldn't expect me to just leave. I had driven fifteen hundred miles to be with her. I turned to Terra Lenda for help but she was walking away. If this was a dream, it was a nightmare.

Alana spun around on her heels. I had never seen her face so ugly. "I told you to leave!" she shrieked.

I didn't know what to do or how to break the spell. "Alana, please," I pleaded. "If I have done something wrong, I am very sorry about it. Can't we please continue with the day?"

"Leave!"

"Alana, you can't mean that."

"I am very serious. I want you to leave and go back to California where you came from."

"To California?" I was devastated by the idea.

"Yes."

I lowered my eyes in an effort to compose myself. I couldn't very well return to California in this mental state. I couldn't go on living my life without understanding what had happened and reconciling with Alana.

I raised my eyes again. Tears streamed down my face and I began to sob. "I can't leave like this, Alana. If I hurt you, I'm sorry. I didn't mean to hurt you. I would never want to hurt you. I love you. You are my teacher and I am bound to you."

"If it is as you say, then you will do as I ask," she said. "You will leave."

"I can't!" I sobbed, "Please don't send me away."

Alana let out a sigh. "If I let you stay, will you do what I ask of you?"

I nodded and tried to control myself. Tears were still rushing down my face making the jagged cliffs around us fade deeper into the background. "Yes, I promise."

Alana reached down to the ground and lifted a huge rock. She hesitated a moment as if to size up its weight, and then she handed it to me. It must have been thirty or forty pounds "Go put this under the front wheel of the Jeep," she said without expression.

The Jeep was more than two miles away. It wasn't on unsteady ground and it didn't need a rock behind the wheel and, even if it did, there were plenty of rocks nearby to accomplish the job. I also knew the task was punishment and that if I argued I would have to leave the ranch. I looked Alana directly in the eyes and then quickly looked away. Cradling the boulder in my arms, I turned and slowly started back, out of the hollow down the hill.

The weight of the boulder gradually overpowered me. I could only carry it a short distance before I had to rest. Sometimes I was able to find ledges to lean it on but, as I progressed along the narrow, steep grade, I was forced to drop it to the ground. Each time I dropped it, it seemed heavier and more of a struggle to lift until finally, I could barely lift it at all. I tried rolling it with my foot but it would invariably end up in an impossible position and I would have to maneuver it free with my hands. My arms and back became painfully strained and it wasn't until several hours later that I finally made it to the bottom of the hill.

I placed the rock under the wheel of the Jeep as directed and went into the house. My shirt was torn in several places and, upon pushing up the sleeves to examine my arms, I found numerous cuts, scrapes and bruises on the inside of my forearms. I went into the bathroom and washed before spreading some salve on the cuts, then I changed shirts and was about to lie down to rest when I heard a noise outside. I went into the kitchen and looked out the window, thinking that Alana had followed me, but saw no one. Then I caught a glimpse of a man, darting in and out of the shadows, as if he was trying to sneak up on the house. Was the man, Bull?

My heart began to race as I watched the man traversing the shadows, as an animal stalks a prey. He would come closer and then stop in the deepest part of a shadow and then approach the house again. Alana's warning that Bull was not in his right mind reminded me of the protection stick she had given me and I was aware that I no longer had it; that I must have dropped it somewhere between the house and the hollow while I struggled with the boulder.

Suddenly, Bull stepped into the open at the back of the house and seemingly stared right at me. He was not a big man but stocky in build, like an gorilla, and he had a knife in his hand. I ducked behind the bedroom curtain, hopeful that he had not seen me, then hurried through the house and bolted out the front door.

I ran at full speed, without looking back, without consciousness of my pain and fatigue, through the meadow, up the deer trail and into the hollow. Only then did I pause to catch my breath.

A doe and her fawn were grazing nearby. Alarmed by my sudden entrance and rasping breath, they started to run off, then settled down a short distance to my left. When I looked, I saw Terra Lenda, the woman in the buckskin dress seated on a huge boulder in the center of the meadow. I started to go over to her when my foot struck an object. Glancing to the ground, I saw that it was the protection stick Alana had given me. I picked it up and then continued toward the woman.

"Hello," Terra Lenda called out as I approached.

"Hello, Terra," I answered, trying to sound as calm as possible. "Is Alana nearby?"

"Yes, Heather, she's with the horses," Terra answered. She looked at me for a long moment. "Sit down with me, Heather."

I looked around to be sure that Bull was nowhere in sight and then took a seat on a rock across from her.

Terra eyed me from my shoes to the top of my head. "This is not an easy time for you, Heather, a very difficult time indeed. I want you to know that I am sorry for you."

The sympathy in her voice made me feel like crying and so, to avoid it, I looked away.

"There is a way to cut through your hardship."

I looked at her again as if to say, "What way?" but I did not speak.

Terra rose to her feet and placed a hand lightly on my shoulder. She looked down, directly into my eyes. "You must become the student Alana asks you to be."

"I try," I said. "I don't know how to be any more of a student to her."

"You must give yourself to her," Terra said softly, "totally give yourself."

Tears came into my eyes and this time I did not look away. Believing I had already given myself to Alana, there seemed nothing more I could give.

Terra stood erect and looked down at me. A gentle breeze lifted the feathers on her buckskin dress and the crystals around her neck danced in the shifting light giving her the appearance of one about to fly. She started to speak and then held a finger to her lips as if listening to something. "Someone's coming," she said, "It's a man..."

I jumped to my feet and clutched the protection stick in the palm of my hand.

"You'd better go," Terra said, but before she had finished speaking I had begun to run toward the hills ahead.

CHAPTER 3
RECEIVING A POWER NAME

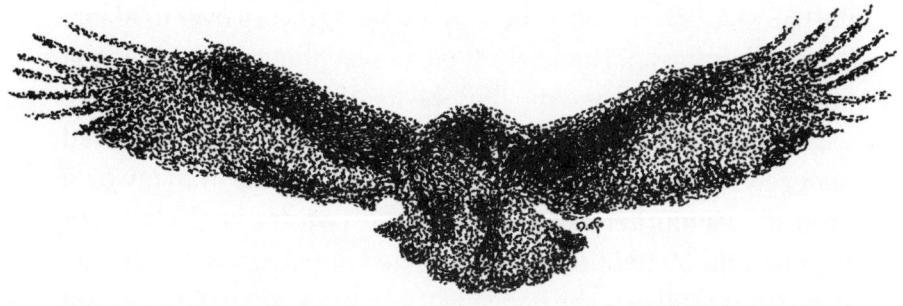

There was no sound at all and, as I looked around at the trees, mountains and skyline, there seemed to be an emptiness, as if everything alive had left. I shifted my weight uneasily against the smooth rock wall behind me. The strained muscles in my arms were no longer numb and they ached in sharp sequence to the raw flesh on my inside forearms. I placed my protection stick across my lap and rolled up my sleeves. The series of cuts and bruises had become uniform welts, like wide-banded stripes along the inside of my arms. They hurt to the touch but moreover they hurt when I moved my arms. I hunched forward and closed my eyes, gently rocking myself in an effort to ease the pain. I didn't know when in my life I had ever felt so tired. I was drained of energy, as though a plug had been yanked and my vitality wasted away. The tension of the day had taken its toll on me —Alana's rejection and then Bull's angry pursuit. I could run no more. I didn't care what happened.

I leaned back against the rock wall and tried to rest. At first I closed my eyes and then I opened them again to gaze into the valley and contemplate the stillness. Nothing at all moved. There was no breeze and the silence was infinite.

I recalled Terra Lenda's words to me, that I could cut through the hardships of my apprenticeship by giving myself over to Alana. What did she mean? I had already given everything of myself. Alana dominated my land and my life. She treated me as an idiot child, telling me what to do, what to say, and what to think. I had followed her every request, even to the point of staying away from my own property without her permission to return. I wrote a book about our relationship. In addition, I traveled the United States to conduct seminars on subjects she had taught me. What more did she want of me? What more of myself could I give? I had no personal life outside of my relationship with her.

An occasional hawk flew beneath the swiftly sailing clouds, flying around the hollow to the other side of the cliffs where I supposed Alana was working with the horses.

I wanted to erase the negative events of the day, to be with her and the horses. I wanted to have time to relax with her; to share with her the events and the conquests of the last year, my experiences and what I learned.

"Alana," I shouted to the hills, "why couldn't you have given me that? Why do you have to create such difficulty about everything in your presence? You seem to be like a spider, always spinning on a web, totally unpredictable. As soon as I become comfortable in your presence, you change. I never know what to expect."

I fell silent again to remember something Alana had once told me. She was explaining that I had mood swings, what she called "mood flip-flops." She claimed that she never had mood flip-flops and that I should be more like her. As I thought about the way she had treated me, she didn't seem constant to me. I wondered if she wasn't a schizophrenic, trying to convince me that it was me who had the problem and not she. I knew that in the eyes of the world, I would be considered the more normal and yet, she had me believing that I should be more like her. She was unlike anyone I had ever known. One moment she had been joking with Terra Lenda about my seriousness, mocking me, and the next she was telling me to get out and go back to California. As I recalled the incident, how I had tried to make light of her mockery by tapping her on the shoulder, to tell her to stop, I became very thirsty and a heaviness settled around my heart.

I thought about why I had tapped Alana on the shoulder. An image of Alana taunting me at the movie theatre came to mind, and her accusation that I was schizophrenic. The memory was followed by another in the morning when she insisted that we hurry to the hollow before I had even brushed my teeth. Then there was a meeting with the mythical Terra and talk about an angry young man named Bull and teasing about who was Indian and who was not.

My concentration was interrupted as I sat up and looked around to confirm what I already knew. If Bull had lived his life in these hills, there was no way he would not find me if he wanted to.

I glanced at the stick Alana had given me and turned it around in my hand. I had an impulse to throw it away and, for an instant, I held it above my head and was ready to pitch it when I lowered my hand again. Never had I discarded anything Alana had given me. To do so now would seem to further weaken our bond and, while I couldn't explain it to myself, I didn't want to let go of her.

My mouth was dry and I realized how thirsty I was. It greatly added to my discomfort.

I closed my eyes and focused on Alana, recalling that she had said that she was Lakota, a Sioux medicine woman. She was going to say something else when I tapped her on the shoulder.

I opened and closed my eyes again. Why hadn't Alana inquired about Spirit, the horse she had given me? Why, from the moment she saw me, did she emotionally push me? Perhaps she hadn't wanted me to return to the ranch. Perhaps she had wanted the place all for herself. Now that I had returned, I was in the way. Why did she suddenly tell me to leave? Wasn't my tap on her shoulder to tell her to take notice of my feelings and to "cut out" that which I didn't like?

A slow chill started in the calf of my legs and rose up my spine as I realized the anger in what I had done. I had hit her lightly but, all the same, I struck her; and, as simple as I felt the tap to be, it was an act of violence. Even though what I had done was considered playfully acceptable to our society, to Alana, I had struck my teacher.

Like the passage of a cloud blocking the sun, the realization slowly illuminated me. A deliberate hit, such as the one I had given Alana, stimulates reaction. Wasn't that the way arguments begin between individuals in our society, and wasn't it the way wars begin between nations? I realized why Alana had been so hard on me.

A hawk screeched overhead. I looked up to acknowledge the sign of a universal agreement that Alana had taught me to recognize and, as I did, my attention was caught not by a hawk, but by an eagle in low flight. The giant bird flew so close that our eyes met and, as it did, I seemed to be drawn into it, as though its wings flapped in rhythm to my heart. My breath caught and I leapt to my feet. As it rose in flight, I sensed that I rose with it, into the wild, blue yonder, the ever-thinning air clearing my mind so that I perceived color and form with added dimension and precision splendor. I was inside of the eagle, looking out at the world, soaring above the mountains from a 360 degree viewpoint.

I was more alive and free feeling than I had ever been in my entire life. The motion of wings wrapped around me made my body weightless, ultra balanced in the high, thin air. I soared over the valley, seeing in every direction, watching deer, rabbit and other bush animals scurrying about on the ground. I flew over the ranch house and saw that there was no one there and then I flew over the meadow where I had been with Terra Lenda but she had gone and there was no sign of Bull either. I flew over the trees and saw hawks nesting and then I rose higher, to the top of the highest mountain, hovering above the craggy surface of it.

And then I saw what I wanted to see. There, on top, nestled in a crevice of the rock, was a huge nest. Hovering above it, I looked to the left and right of the great wings that lifted me and, in response to a thought I held, they fluttered, then floated me down, like a single feather floating from a height, and landed me on top of it. The thick matted grass cushioned my body, then molded itself to me as I felt myself relax.

I pampered and preened myself, removing bits of debris that had collected in the hinges of my wings. When I was finished, I gently plucked a feather from my tail and inwardly commanded the great eagle form that enveloped me to rise back into the sky.

In one great sweep of wings we were sailing the skies. I was about to circle the mountain to search for Alana, when I looked down and saw myself standing on the ground with my arms outstretched overhead. Alana stood a few feet behind me.

As I identified myself with the figure below, I was drawn down, pushed down suddenly with tremendous force, like a rock gaining speed as it falls from a cliff, and with a terrible jolt, the part of me that flew was back in my body again. After a moment, I turned around.

Alana looked at me with tears in her eyes. "Heather," she said softly, "show me what it is that you hold in your hand."

I held up the feather I had plucked from the eagle's tail and, astounded by the validation of what I had experienced, offered it to Alana, recalling the day we had met, driving out to my Uncle Farley's ranch. That day I had turned to ask her something and had seen an eagle reflected in her eyes.

"Do not give your eagle feather to me, Heather. It belongs to you. Do you understand?"

I remained looking into her eyes and could not speak.

"You have discovered a part of your medicine power," Alana said softly.

"You are an eagle medicine woman," I said in an uncertain voice.

Alana shook her head. "No, Heather it is you who are the eagle!" A tear overflowed from her eyes and slipped down the side of her face. "You must never again attempt to give away your power. You must make that promise now. There is nothing more endangering to you." She paused, squinting at me as if to see me more clearly. "Do you know what gives the eagle its power?"

Still unable to speak, I shook my head.

"What gives the eagle its power is its superb sight, not its talons. Vision is the ability to rise above the situation and 'read' it accurately. Your flight today contains all the information you need to know about your life, only it may take you years to contemplate it."

For a moment, Alana remained silent as though lost in thought.

"To the Lakota people, you are 'winged wolf,' which, in the ancient language, means eagle."

"Why is it that a wolf is called an eagle?" I asked.

Alana went on. "A wolf, like an eagle, is a teacher and a pathfinder. Wolf is the pathfinder on land and eagle is the pathfinder in the skies. Wolf teaches the secrets of mother earth, while eagle teaches from the heart of the sky. The Great Spirit's voice can be heard in the eagle's cry, whereas the earth mother speaks through the wolf's howl. Both eagle and wolf are loyal and true to their purpose and loved ones throughout their lives. The nature of their lives are the same, except that one is of earth and the other air." Alana examined me from toe to head and then said, "You may be Heather Hughes-Calero to the world, but your true identity is the woman called Winged-Wolf."

I was speechless, overcome with a new sense of myself, a being that had found its identity and was recognizing itself. I was a winged wolf in a woman's body. I had found my power animal, which meant in American Indian that I had found the symbols that represented the evolution of my soulself, and defined the nature and medicine of the weaknesses and strengths that I would deal with during my lifetime. Together they would help me understand the initiation that life was giving me. "I will honor my name," I said softly, finding some effort in speaking aloud.

"Now you will come to understand why it is so difficult for us to work together, Heather; so difficult for you to understand me." She looked down in the valley and then back at me again. "We are very different. You see things always from a great height, often forgetting you are a physical being who needs nurturing from the earth. Your food comes from creatures who walk the earth, yet you are always drawn upward, away from life." She hesitated as if to make her point more pronounced. "Even though you are not an earth creature, you may not lose contact with it. If you do, your life will be of no purpose. Do you understand me?"

"But the wolf side of my nature brings me in touch with the earth," I said.

"It will, but it hasn't," Alana said. "Until now, your wolf nature has been underdeveloped. That is why I have sent you out into the world to teach others of the earth mother. You are becoming grounded to the earth but you are not, as yet, a hundred percent. When you give yourself totally up to her, you will be free to live as you wish on the earth and in the sky. Your near and far vision will then illuminate the path for others. Do you understand me?"

I nodded that I did, mesmerized by what she was telling me.

Alana appeared deep in thought, studying me. "I have been trying to teach you to ground yourself here, to the earth. Once grounded, you can soar to any height and return with a feather." She paused again. "Your role in life is to write and to teach others, Heather. Your medicine will empower you." She hesitated, then asked, "You believe that I am of horse medicine, don't you?"

I nodded that I did.

She shook her head. "No, Heather. I am great friends with horses but they are not my real medicine power." She placed an arm about my shoulder and led me to the stone seat next to the cliff wall and sat down. I sat on a fallen tree trunk opposite her. "I am a Lakota badger medicine woman, Heather."

"Lakota badger?" I repeated, unsure of what she was trying to tell me.

"Lakota is what my people call themselves. It is an Indian word. The white man calls us Sioux."

Although she had previously told me that she was not Indian, I was not surprised to learn that she was, and this time in the telling, I knew she wasn't teasing.

"I am of badger medicine," she said again. "Do you know what that means?"

I hesitated, scrutinously thinking about what I knew about badgers, which wasn't much. I had heard they were animals that lived in holes, under tree roots, and that, if provoked, they had a reputation of picking on others, badgering them.

Alana had been watching my reaction and she now burst out laughing. "Do I fit the description?" she asked impishly.

I looked away, to the soft sandy floor beneath where we sat and smoothed the eagle feather in my hand. I did not know what to say. While I had never considered it, the idea that she was badger medicine made a great deal of sense to me, and I suddenly understood why she treated me in such a gruff way.

"You realize now why I am so strict with you, so difficult a teacher?" She hesitated before continuing. "It is my nature. While the badger can be gentle, there isn't a creature on earth who wishes to rub the fur of the badger the wrong way." She paused in a way that forced me to look her directly in the eyes. "Because I am a medicine woman, Heather, I work from the heart. At times you have complained because of the love flow that you felt from me. Be grateful."

I laughed nervously. She had indeed been hard on me. My scarred arms were additional proof of that, but she had forced me to step forward in spite of my rebellion and I was grateful to her for it.

"As a medicine woman, I am dedicated to my work and steadfast to the end, except when I know there is no longer purpose to my work."

"There is purpose between us," I said quickly. "I know how difficult a student I am, but I have learned much from you."

She smiled. "I know you have, but I want you to know that there are easier ways...for both of us. Someone of more compatible medicine could make it so much easier for you."

As always, I couldn't bear the thought of losing her and I suddenly realized why. "I think I needed your abrasiveness, Alana. Other teachers I have had in life have not been able to open me to the degree that you have. You are a gift from the divine consciousness and I want to keep you as my teacher. From the opposition of your mind to mine, I have learned what I have never before learned. You have shifted my viewpoint 360 degrees. Life is so different for me than it was before we met. You have directed my energies to accomplish my destiny. You have made me aware of living life."

I then told Alana how sorry I was for hitting her on the shoulder and what I understood from the incident, the subtle reflection of argument and war. I did not mention my struggle to carry the rock that she asked me to place at the wheel of the Jeep, nor did I comment on the soreness in my arms.

"Soon your anger will leave you and then you will not care what I do to you." Alana had a faraway look in her eyes, as though she was deep in thought, then she brightened. "Ah, Terra," she said quickly rising.

I turned to see Terra Lenda step into the alcove, conscious of the feathers that fringed her clothing, and rose to my feet as well. She was a strange looking woman, sharp but gentle features and there was a glow to her skin like my own. "Terra, will you show Heather where to find water so she can clean her teeth," Alana said lightly.

I looked at her, amazed that she knew my thoughts so well. She had known that I had been angry about not being able to brush my teeth.

Alana smiled. "Then you can bring her to me. I will be with the horses."

As I left with Terra Lenda, I reached down and plucked a length of bear grass from the ground and began to strip it into a thin thread. As we walked, I used the thread to lash my eagle feather to the protection stick that Alana had given me. I knew I was safe from Bull for the time-being.

CHAPTER 4

LEARNING ABOUT 'MATCHING ENERGIES'

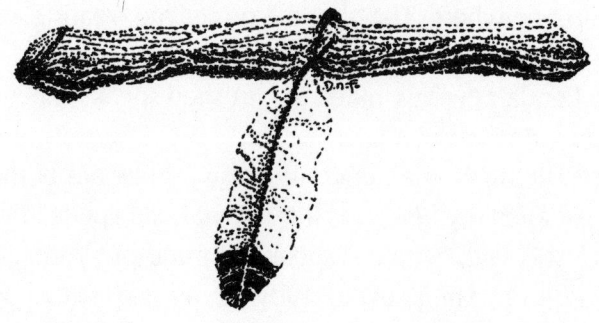

Terra Lenda led me along a steep narrow trail around the base of the mountain and stopped beneath a protrusion of rock. Underneath was a large round pool of water about the size of a small pond. It was in an area that I hadn't bothered exploring, which explained to me why I didn't know it was there.

"It's the community drinking hole," Terra said, reflecting on my surprise. "All the wildlife know of it." She turned and pointed to the intersecting animal trails that ended there. "And it's clean, fed from underground springs."

I knew that Colorado mountain water was clean and clear and so, without hesitation, I leaned down and placed my lips on the surface of the water and took a long drink. When I had finished I turned around. Terra had seated herself a short distance away, looking at me. Her eyes were bright with amusement.

I smiled back. "Do you live near here Terra?"

She didn't answer.

I sat gazing into her eyes, thinking of the question I had asked her and, as I did, it seemed as though I was inside her speaking aloud an answer to myself. "I am Terra Lenda, which means energy matcher. I am you. I am Alana. I am all those who communicate with me. I live in the minds of others as a reflection. My home is in everyone, everywhere. The clothes you see me wearing, represent your vision of me."

Terra Lenda's eyes twinkled as I finished speaking her answer. "Now you know who I am," she said.

I stared at the woman uncomfortably, uncertain of the words that had escaped my lips. Was it true that I had spoken her mind?

"Yes," she said, "you did speak my mind but you also spoke your own mind." She paused, studying my perplexity. "Heather, you cannot know my thoughts unless the seed of them resonates in you."

I stared at the crystals hanging in the center of her chest. I noticed for the first time that a feather hung in the center of them, not a hawk feather but distinctly a white and brown feather, identical to the one I had taken from the eagle.

"What troubles you?" she asked.

I was confused and could not speak.

"You must tell me."

"Surely, you must know," I answered.

"You challenge me because you do not trust me," Terra said, "but moreover, you do not trust yourself. You want to know why I wear an eagle feather and yet you already know why, because what you see in me is your own vision. You are the eagle, Heather."

I was dumbfounded and could think of nothing sensible to say. After a few moments, I asked, "Have you lived in these hills long?"

Terra smiled. "I live where the seeker on the threshold lives. I am the mirror for all who need to see themselves. I am an illusion reflecting your reality."

Although I had hoped for a reasonable answer, I managed to ask, "Why would I use you as a mirror instead of Alana?"

"Oh, you use her plenty." Terra laughed. "When you found the eagle feather, didn't you suppose that she was of eagle medicine?"

"Yes," I answered, not thinking that believing Alana to be of eagle medicine was using her.

"Well then, you see what I mean," she added lightly. "You use others to express yourself." She paused, studying me. I was about to object when she added, "People use each other to express themselves, Heather. They see something in a person because they see it in themselves and they naturally suppose that the other person is the same as themselves. In reality, only the energy is the same but they feel by matching it, it is the same."

I was thoroughly confused and said so.

"Haven't you ever looked at someone and felt you knew them?" Terra asked.

"Yes," I answered thoughtfully, thinking of all the people in my life I felt close to.

"What you felt was that you and the other individual had some similar energy and in the moment of meeting those energies were matched to reflect each other like a tiny mirror. As a result, you felt you really had something in common with that person, which you did." She rose to her feet and leaned back against the rock wall at the opposite end of the pool. A hawk screeched in the distance. I recognized it as a sign that the hawk, Terra's medicine animal, was in agreement.

"It's how bonds develop between people, Heather."

I was thoughtful, wondering about the bond that I felt with Alana.

"You want to know why Alana is your teacher?" Terra asked.

"We are all teachers to each other," I answered, wanting her to know that I was not entirely ignorant of spiritual principles.

"It is true that we are all teachers to each other," she said, "but we are talking about energy-matches and the type of energy-match that makes one a teacher and another a student."

I waited for her to go on.

"A medicine woman, or man, is neither Indian or non-Indian."

"I know that!" I injected.

"Good. Then you also realize a medicine woman, or man, is not bound to the rules of 'this medicine or that'?"

I nodded. "To me, Alana seems to be all medicines," I said respectfully.

"That is because she is whole," Terra said. "A medicine woman is not limited by viewpoint. A medicine woman is one who shape shifts to become what her student needs her to be, and yet she has her own individual nature, which designates her power medicine. For me it is the hawk, for Alana the badger and for you it is the winged-wolf."

Alana had explained to me that the eagle-wolf was my medicine and I thought I understood.

"You do not understand," Terra said, glaring at me. "She has so much trouble with you because you always think that you do understand, when you don't."

I lowered my eyes and recalled on a previous visit when Alana had told me I was a bad student because I was filled with preconceived ideas and opinions about everything. When she talked to me, I always believed I understood. She had said that the only way to be a good student was to approach the teacher empty and without opinion.

"Are all medicine women energy matchers like yourself?" I asked.

Terra's expression softened. "Y - e - s," she answered slowly, "but it is also my own individual nature. It is my role in life."

"What do you mean?" I prodded.

"What do you see?"

A hawk dipped down from the cliffs and danced about Terra's head. Watching me watch it she burst out laughing.

"I don't get it," I said, concerned that the bird was going to excrete while it was hovering. Suddenly it landed on her shoulder and folded its wings. Her eyes widened as if to say, "Did you get it?"

"I already know you are hawk medicine," I said.

"Yes, but do you know what hawk medicine means?"

I had done some studying on the meaning of different Indian medicine animals and so I said, "You are a messenger."

She smiled again. "What is the message I carry, Heather?"

"I don't know."

"Yes, you do."

"Hawk medicine reminds one to be observant," I said thoughtfully, "to observe the obvious. It says that life is sending signals."

"Yes." Terra fell silent again, looking at me in a way that emphasized that I should think on the answer I had given. I thought of Alana's treatment of me, how sore my arms were from carrying the boulder to the Jeep; of being told to perform at the old movie theatre and then being told I was schizophrenic; and I thought of Bull, who was angry at me without knowing me or the circumstances of my inheritance. Or did he? Did he know why my uncle had left me the ranch? What was the reason? Why was it I knew so little of my uncle to begin with? Why would no one in my family speak of him?

"All of the questions that come to mind are connected to the Hawk's cry for you to pay attention to the signs and the signals around you," Terra said. "Hawk knows because hawk is THE energy matcher." She fell silent again.

I looked up at her, thinking about the events of the day. The tap I had given Alana on the shoulder had brought immediate repercussions, and not only from her. It was shortly after that Bull appeared to threaten me. I told Terra about Bull's appearance with a knife outside the ranch house following the incident with Alana. It seemed to me that when I did something with great feeling, it was like throwing a pebble into the water and having it spiral outward. An effect spiraled outward into the environment and often showed up in reactions of others toward me.

Terra brought her hands together in steepling position. "Yes," she said thoughtfully. "Strong energy draws strong reaction. You know how you felt when you saw Bull...and how you feel now..." She stopped mid-sentence as the sound of a twig snapped nearby. I looked in the direction of the noise, so terrified I could barely breathe and when I looked back to Terra Lenda again, hoping for comfort, she was gone.

I clutched the protection stick to my chest and mumbled a few words of prayer trying to calm my fright, then I made my way around the watering hole and dropped to my knees to crawl through a small animal tunnel at the roots of the thick brush. I decided not to wait to see if it was Bull, but to get out of there and I began to crawl as quietly and as quickly as I could.

It was some time before I came to a clearing and rose to my feet again. I brushed the dirt from my jeans and looked around. Off in the distance a black bear lumbered across the land. I watched him until he was out of sight, and then drew in a deep breath. Here in the mountains, I was above 8,000 feet and, in all of the excitement,

I had neglected to breathe slowly and deeply. I was tired and felt that I would have to rest.

The clearing was round, intersected by trails in each of the four directions. To the north was a small grove of aspens and I went to it and stretched out on a bed of dry leaves in the center of it. In my fatigue, I forgot about my earlier fright and I forgot about Bull. It seemed the events of the day had been blown out of proportion like a bad dream. As I drifted into sleep, I thought of the clearing as a medicine wheel and the aspen grove where I lay as the powerful north fork of the medicine wheel, and I remembered the bear, a symbol of the north. A twig snapped nearby but I did not move. If the bear were to appear I was too tired to care. Another twig snapped amid the sound of rustling leaves. I opened my eyes. The shadow of a great bird soaring above the trees touched me and then flew away as I closed my eyes again. The leaves and the ground beneath it moved as something neared. With my ear to the ground, I listened. While the sound neared, I was surprisingly unafraid. It came closer and closer until I could hear it breathe next to me, and I sensed that whatever it was, it lay down at my side. Very slowly I opened my eyes.

A furry grey-white face with a long, pointed nose was very nearly touching mine. I was surprised at myself for not being startled. As though in a dream, I gazed calmly into the eyes of a dog-like creature lying on its side next to me. The black tip of the animal's nose twitched as though familiarizing itself with my scent and then the animal reached with its tongue to lick my face. I raised a hand to stroke the great grey-white furry head, kneading my fingers into the thick, coarse fur behind its ears. The fur had a familiar feel, as though I had stroked it many times before, and I knew that if what I was experiencing was hallucination, the hallucination was no stranger to me. I was as comfortable with this creature as I was with my household pets and, in some way, even more familiar. It was this naturalness that I felt that made it possible for me to drift into sleep.

I awoke feeling half-starved and chilled by early evening air and sat up. The sun had already dropped behind the mountains. I thought of the animal that had been with me and would have thought it to have been a dream, except that, next to me, the ground was smooth and indented as if a figure half the size of my own had lain there. I stood up and stared down at it, trying to determine the type of animal it could have been, larger than a common dog but smaller than a bear. There were no tracks leading up to it. Off in the distance an animal howled. I looked around. Shadows were deepening, inching their way into the clearing from the base of the cliffs and I became very aware that darkness was coming and that I wasn't certain I knew where I was in relation to the cabin.

I became painfully aware that I hadn't taken the time to eat and I recalled that Alana had said for me to wait and eat with the others. Instead it had been a day of bizarre meetings and spontaneous events.

I went to the edge of the cliff and looked down. The house was directly below me and I decided that I could make it before dark if I hurried.

I stumbled onto the porch and dusted the brush and dirt from my clothes and then entered. Alana was sitting on the couch in front of the fireplace, a spread of vegetables and breads were laid out on the burlwood table in front of her. The fireplace was prepared and ready to light. Alana looked back over her shoulder as I came into the room.

"I thought if you saw smoke from the chimney, you would think it was Bull and be afraid to come home," she said kindly. "But you can light it now, if you want to."

I was aware of the gentleness in her voice and went to the fireplace and struck a match, then touched it to the paper under a tepee of kindling that Alana had prepared. When I had finished, I turned to face Alana. The memory of looking into the furry face of the animal that had lain with me returned.

"Sit down and eat something," Alana said, motioning me to sit next to her on the couch. She rose from her seat as I sat down and went into the kitchen. A moment later she returned with a steaming bowl of vegetable stew. Its aroma filled the room. She placed the bowl in front of me and sat down again. "Eat, Heather, and then we'll talk." She watched me as I ate hungrily. When I had finished, she rose from her seat again and went to stoke the fire, then stood in front of the rising flames to warm her backside.

"Why did you come to Colorado?" she asked.

I marveled at her timing. I had just finished the last spoonful of vegetable stew and had placed the bowl on the table when she asked the question. I leaned with my back against the couch to think about what to answer. Up until this point I had told myself that I had come back to show her our first finished book and to tell her that I had been carrying out her request of me to lecture and teach in the world. Now I knew there was a greater reason. I had returned because I needed to be a student again.

"I have nothing to give if I am not learning," I said, wishing I had chosen better words. "I'm always learning, I know that," I added awkwardly.

"I sent you away because you were becoming addicted to me," Alana said, not unkindly. "Because you needed time to be alone in your resistance. Addiction is resistance to something and hanging onto it at the same time." She sighed. "And you have not recuperated from it yet. When you left me, you had reached a plateau in your apprenticeship with me. You had learned something and you needed time to express it before continuing. Instead, you were impatient and returned before your time. You never really let go."

I was uncertain about what she was trying to tell me and I told her so.

"You do not understand because you do not belong with me," Alana said firmly. "You listen to my words like you listen to some news on the radio. You think I am giving you bits of information, while in reality I am giving you a way of seeing life."

I leaned forward and asked her to explain.

"Your mind is too strong, Heather." She moved away from the fire and sat in a wooden rocker across from me. I knew she was not giving me a compliment, that in saying my mind was too strong, she was saying that she could not get through to me.

"Perhaps you could say it in another way," I said sincerely.

Alana shook her head. "How, Heather?"

I hesitated, then said that she shouldn't worry, that life would teach me.

"Life is THE initiation, Heather, which means that every action is a performance of consciousness." She paused to see that I was following her. "You still do not see that, not really. You think you do, but you don't."

"How will I know when I do?" I asked. Every so often I could glimpse at the meaning of life as an initiation, at myself as Soul acting in a physical body.

Alana's face seemed to change as I waited for her to answer. "You will know," she said. "You will know when you look at everything in life as a sign, and as a signal and warning of what is going on inside of you. When you realize you can shape-shift and do so to adapt to the forces around you." She narrowed her eyes and leaned forward, staring at me. "You will know when you are your own lawmaker, when you can shift into the shape of the moment, into every experience."

I reflected on the memory of the furry face that had lain next to me and I told her of the experience, how I had grown tired and how it seemed that the animal had lain down next to me, and that I was unafraid.

Alana remained silent as though she was replaying my story over again in her mind, then she began a slow backward-forward motion in her rocker.

"Is that what you meant by calling me schizophrenic?" I asked, uneasy by her silence. So much had happened in the past twenty-four hours, beginning with my command performance on stage at Smith's Theater.

"No! You are becoming less and less schizophrenic every day, Heather. I told you that a schizophrenic person is one who thinks and does one thing while feeling another. There is a conflict between how a schizophrenic lives and how they want to live. Many people function with a fractured personality because they don't feel they have a right to live as they wish. More and more you are living as you want to live. You are living for yourself, Heather and, in living for yourself, you are learning that you have much to give to people."

I was encouraged by her praise of me and asked what I could do to better my relationships within the world.

She sighed and said nothing for a long time. "Be yourself, Heather. Be yourself in every way that you can. It is the impeccable way of medicine women and men."

I was about to ask her how one knew when they were "being themselves" and how they knew when they were acting out of social pressure. I explained that many times it seemed that the two roads merged and narrowed into a fine line and I had difficulty differentiating my feelings from another's.

Alana sat forward in her chair and stopped rocking. "When you feel uncomfortable, uneasy or in pain; when you feel in a hurry to solve problems, under pressure, crowded, or anxious and there seems to be a lot of noise around you; you are being affected by the feelings and desires of what others want from you." She paused, studying me. I felt I knew exactly what she was saying and I nodded my head in agreement. While I had never thought of what she had told me in exactly those terms, I immediately recognized the uncomfortable feelings she was talking about.

"When everything seems fine," Alana went on, "when you feel comfortable and you don't feel that you owe anyone anything, you are one with yourself." She squinted her eyes and pinched her lips together as if she was examining me. "Do you remember the method of using soft vision I taught you?"

"Yes," I answered, recalling how she had had me following her through the mountains using my peripheral vision. I had written about soft seeing in *Woman Between the Wind*. "I remember."

"When you are soft-seeing, you are seeing the world from the center of your head," Alana added. "Seeing the world from the center of your head means that you are looking at life from the viewpoint of soul. You are then living life from consciousness and not merely from the brain." She narrowed her eyes at me again and then sat back in her chair and relaxed. A light smile upturned the corners of her mouth. "There was a time that I told you, you had no inner voice, that what you thought was inner voice was really nothing more than mind chatter, but I can see that you have changed."

In some ways I felt that what she said was true, that I was perceiving experiences rather than analyzing them, but there were still times when I knew I got caught up in mulling things over too much.

"I have been hard on you...I know," Alana said in a soft voice, watching me.

"No, that's not it, Alana." I became quiet and suddenly aware of the scrapes and bruises on my arms. Quite unexpectedly, tears began streaming down my face. I knew I was reacting to Alana pitying me.

"You haven't asked me much about Terra Lenda, or Bull," Alana said.

I picked up my protection stick, with the eagle feather still lashed to it, and laid it across my lap.

Alana watched me. "Is there something you would like me to tell you about them?" she asked.

I shook my head. While I had many questions, I didn't have the energy to ask them.

"Have you been playing the stone game?" Alana asked.

I told her that I had, that I used the game as a teaching tool in my workshops. It was a game she had taught me to develop and refine companion energy. I reminded her that I had written about the game in *Woman Between the Wind.*

"Seems there is nothing to teach you," she said, grinning.

"I would like to know more about companion energy, in particular matching energies."

"Your experience with the eagle and with the furry faced animal were both examples of matching energies," Alana said. "The merger of identities is now complete. You have met the eagle and the wolf as well."

"You mean, the creature that slept next to me was the winged-wolf?"

"The earth mother introduced you in a way that you could accept introduction."

"It was a white wolf," I said, remembering.

Alana nodded soberly, "I know, I saw it in a dream." she said. "Its color changes the sound of your name and its meaning."

"In what way?"

Alana leaned back in her rocker and tapped the palms of her hands together. "Your name now becomes Winged White-Wolf," she said. "While a white wolf is still a wolf, it is a phantom beast that lives upon the earth of many dimensions. It is a special totem, but special does not mean good but rather extraordinary, and being extraordinary can be very difficult."

I was perplexed and told her so.

"It was good you came back," Alana said. "You were ready to come back." She rose from her seat and slowly walked to the door, opening it. I followed her. She turned to face me. "Tomorrow, when you awaken, I want you to go to the hollow and help me with the horses."

"I'd love to!"

"Good." She turned to go and then turned back again. "Don't worry, Bull will not disturb you tonight," she said.

With a sigh of relief, I said goodnight and watched her disappear into the darkness.

CHAPTER 5
DECISION-MAKING

When I reached the hollow, Alana was already there, her body bent, her ear against the belly of a mare. I approached her as quietly as I could so as not to disturb her and frighten the horse but, even though her back was toward me, she seemed to know I was there and turned to me.

"Good morning, Alana," I said in a soft voice.

She smiled in greeting, which put me at ease. It was not usual for Alana to smile when she saw me. She continued running her hand along the mare's belly. "Come here," she called.

I did as she asked and placed a hand on the mare's belly next to hers. Something moved to my touch. It moved again. I knew the mare was with foal.

"Do you see how low she is carrying her baby?" Alana asked.

"Yes," I answered and stood back to study the slope of the mare's abdomen.

"I want you to observe how the mare moves." Alana said. She

turned and stood at the horse's shoulder, dipped her head and shoulders and began to walk forward. The mare walked in unison with her. "Do you see anything unusual?" she called back to me.

I watched as Alana and the mare moved across the field. The mare seemed stiff and awkward in its forelegs. I mentioned this to her.

"Good!" Alana left the mare and walked back over to me. "The mare will deliver today," she said. "She has three signs. The first two you noticed. One was the lowness of abdomen and the other, the shift of the foal in her abdomen. But the third you could only realize if you had matched her energy and shape-shifted into her." She paused, studying me.

I didn't know what to say and remained quiet.

She smiled and I knew she was pleased with me for not arguing the idea or chatting idly.

"You are aware that I am pleased with you because, at this moment, you are matching energy with me. For an instant, when I explained my energy matching with the mare, you shape-shifted and became me."

I was amazed and said nothing.

"You shape-shifted with the eagle and you became it," Alana said, eyeing me. "You shape-shifted again with a white wolf and you were able to sleep next to it." She paused and then added, "and you shape-shifted with Bull. Your anger at me for having you carry the boulder to the Jeep matched Bull's anger at you for enjoying his house. Bull then came at you because of the anger you were carrying inside of yourself." She hesitated, then added, "As you can see, if you are not conscious and in control of yourself every minute, matching energy can present peculiar circumstances."

I was still too astounded to speak. If what she said was true, and deep down I knew it was, then energy-matching or shape-shifting was something that everyone did every time they came in contact with another person. It explained why we feel different in the presence of one person than another.

"Yes," Alana said as if listening to my thoughts. "Shape-shifting is the very essence of communication. When we are trying to understand another person's idea or we try to get them to understand ours, we shape-shift with that individual; that is, we make the effort to match energies with them. It is through this process of matching-energies that we become one with someone or something. If the energies do not match, there is poor communication and you feel uncomfortable or you make someone else feel uncomfortable. The same is true with being in the presence of animals or even places."

"How so with places?" I asked.

"When you walk into a place and feel at home, it is because the energies there are compatible," Alana said, "and if they're not compatible, you can change them. If you hang around long enough in a place, it will take on your energies, providing there are not stronger energies for it to feed upon."

"You mean environments feed on energy?" I asked.

"Yes. Life is energy," Alana answered. "The lesser energy always yields to the greater energy. But energy matching between people or animals is done successfully, not in one overpowering the other, but in finding a common ground where both can co-exist. Now we're talking about true companion energy."

Alana had said so much that I needed to pause and absorb and I told her how I felt.

"Don't worry," she said. "Today you will learn about shape-shifting, through your own experience, but first we must make sure the mare is safe to deliver her foal." Alana moved away from me and went to the mare and, standing at the horse's shoulder, she lowered her head. The mare lowered her head as well and moved in step with her. I followed.

Alana led the way to a small box canyon that had been specially prepared with a thick carpet of clean dry grasses. Off to one side was a large wooden container of dried corn and oats and another of water. After she saw that the mare was contenting herself, she turned to me to indicate it was time to leave. I thought Alana would seal off the entrance to the box canyon to confine the mare but she didn't. I asked her about it.

"The mare knows why she is there," Alana explained. "She has everything she needs and, if help is required, we will return."

I was pleased by her usage of the term "we" and asked if the mare knew she was all right by means of energy matching with Alana.

"We have communicated," Alana said, "and you are right, our means of communication was through energy-matching. The mare is in agreement that we will work together to ensure a safe birth for her foal. If she needs me, I will be there. So you see she has no reason to leave the canyon and I have no reason to confine her." She paused and looked deeply into me. For a moment my whole body tingled and I was sure she was energy-matching with me. She smiled as though in agreement. "All this time, since we first met, I have been trying to realign your assemblage point so that we could work together in companion energy. It is easy with an animal because they live by their instincts, whereas most humans have lost their instincts. Most are operating from mind chatter, thinking about this, thinking about that; always mulling everything over. There can be no companion energy with one who is entrapped by the mind."

Alana walked a few feet and then turned to me to ask for my protection stick.

I handed it to her, noting that the eagle feather was securely tied to its center.

Alana held the stick by the ends in front of me. "There are two ends to the stick," she said, fingering both ends. "One is thought, mind, and the other is consciousness or soul. You have to learn which end to choose and when to choose it." She glared at me as if to caution me to pay strict attention. "There are times when we must focus with the mind, when thinking about something is necessary, as well as times when it isn't. When there is nothing that needs thinking about, we must shift into a consciousness state." She paused again and handed me the stick. "Today is the day that you will understand." She began to walk. I trotted along side of her in an effort to keep up. "Find yourself a comfortable rock to hold in the palm of your hand," she instructed, moving ahead of me at a brisk pace.

I stopped and fumbled around on the ground, trying to find a rock but she was getting so far ahead of me that I dropped what I had in my hand and ran to catch up.

"You don't need to crawl around on your hands and knees to find a suitable rock," Alana said. "You can walk with me, as fast as I am going. If you know how to listen to the voices of rocks calling out as we pass, one rock will actually call out to you and ask to serve as your tool. It will catch your eye as it calls to you, but you must be watchful."

Not long ago the idea of a rock calling out to me would have seemed absurd, but not any longer. I looked at the ground as Alana hurried me along toward the far end of the hollow. I saw many rocks but none seemed to call out to me until the hand carrying the stick Alana had given me relaxed at my side. It was then that a pinkish-white rock caught my eye and I stopped and picked it up. "This is it," I said.

Alana stopped and came back to where I stood.

I showed her the rock I had found and explained that it seemed that when the stick I was carrying was pointed at the ground, was when I finally found it.

Alana's eyes glittered with pleasure. "Good job," she said. "The rock you found matched energy, not only with you, but with the task that it is to perform."

I didn't know what she was talking about and waited for her to continue.

"You are to use the rock to polish the stick to a high finish," Alana said. "The polishing will take some time but, when you are finished, both the rock and the stick will be your friends and both will have taught you much about yourself, as well as about true companion energy."

I hesitated.

"What don't you understand?

"How energy matching takes place."

"I told you." She sounded annoyed.

"Okay," I said, not wanting to upset her.

"Don't pretend like you're walking on thin ice around me," Alana snapped. "The image sets you up for a spill in the ice water."

I didn't know what to say and so I remained silent, wishing I hadn't questioned her.

"You're not paying attention," Alana snapped again.

"I don't know what I'm not paying attention to," I answered pathetically.

"I told you that the image of thin ice will set you up for a spill in ice water," she repeated. "I'm trying to explain to you that the image you carry in mind and consciousness predicts the outcome of an energy match. Wasn't that your question?"

I suddenly understood what she was trying to get across. I had been trying to understand what actually happened in an energy match. Alana was explaining that an energy match took place as a result of a mental image.

"There are medicine women who are better suited to be your teacher," Alana said.

I shook my head and began to rub the oblong rock I had found against the side of my protection stick. Alana nodded approvingly and began walking again. I hurried to catch up and then fell into a rhythm of polishing the stick while walking in step with her. I knew that our fluid togetherness was a demonstration of companion energy but I kept quiet about it. I had much to think about, it felt soothing to have something to do with my hands.

"Since you like to think so much, I'll give you something else to think about," Alana said after a while, continuing to walk at a good pace. It seemed she was leading me into another area of the property I had not yet explored and I tried to pay attention to any unusual landmarks along the way.

"The stick is a decision maker," Alana began. "One end of the stick is the valley and the other end the mountain, or one end is cold and the other is hot, or one end is negative and the other positive." She glanced at me to see that I understood and then continued. "The stick also has a middle or balance point. See if you can find that now."

We stopped walking. I slid the stick along the side of my finger until it was balanced, although the point of balance was more to one end than the other, and then looked to Alana for approval.

Alana began to walk again. "The balance point is where you can weigh both sides of a situation or get a detached view of going one way or the other. From this point you will see that the mountain is no greater than the valley. In other words, there is no good end of the stick, and no bad. On the mountain side there is height to look down on a situation and on the valley side there is the ability to see with level eyes what the heights are about." She paused again. "Decide now, which is the mountain side of your stick and which is the valley side."

Alana stood looking over me as I stopped to examined the stick. There was a little knob on one end and I decided that that would be the mountain side and that the narrower end would be the valley. We began walking again.

"Now listen closely," she said. "I am about to tell you how to grab the right end of the stick at a given moment, that is how to make the decision that is best for your life."

I stopped rubbing the stick and looked up at her and then slowly lowered my head again to resume work on the stick. She slowed her walk, which seemed to make it easier for me to concentrate.

"When you have a burning desire to make a particular decision or to grab the opposite end of the stick from which you are holding, know that you are holding the right end."

"What?" I asked, turning to face her, uncertain I had heard her correctly.

A quick smile appeared and then disappeared from her face. "A burning desire to go in a particular direction means that you are sitting in your seat of power and wanting to give it up."

"Huh?" I said stupidly, unable to formulate the barrage of questions rushing to mind.

"Heather, you think that I said that you shouldn't do what you want in life and that is not what I said." She glared at me to be sure that I was paying attention before she continued. "I told you that when you have a consuming desire to do something that you are being led by your emotions and not by your consciousness. If you made such a decision based on your emotions, you would be happy with it for only a very short period of time, until the newness wore off or you saw the end of the path. Consciousness, on the other end, constitutes the true heart of the individual. It provides a path of many choices, intersecting many paths and it never traps one in a stuck situation."

Alana began to walk again at a rapid pace. I had to hurry to catch up.

"The right end of the stick is the one that offers the greatest possibilities," Alana said. She made a sharp turn behind a protrusion of rock and entered a clearing. Terra Lenda and a young man were toiling over a cooking pot some thirty yards ahead. As we neared, the air was filled with the aroma of vegetable and pine nut stew. Terra Lenda turned to greet us while the young man braced himself against a rock next to her. I knew it was Bull, and I also knew I was safe in Alana's presence.

He looked directly at me and then turned his attention to Alana. He smiled as she said something to him, then glanced threateningly at me before he answered her.

I stood next to Terra Lenda and waited for her to look up from the stew she was stirring.

"Do you know why I left you?" Terra asked, turning as she looked up from the stew.

I remembered how Terra had seemingly disappeared when I believed Bull had found me. "No," I answered, shaking my head. I had supposed that there was some lesson to my being left alone.

"Because Heather enjoys her fear and you didn't want to interfere," Alana piped up.

I quickly turned to face her. Bull was walking away from us. "I don't enjoy being afraid," I said in a soft voice not wanting Bull to hear.

"You love your fear!" Alana shot back in a loud voice. Bull seemed to hesitate before continuing to walk away. "You love it so much that you tire me out begging for me to make you afraid."

"I do not!"

"Yes, Heather, you do. It is why you like to visit me. I keep you on edge, afraid for your feelings." Alana paused to glare at me and then burst out laughing.

I was offended and looked to Terra Lenda for sympathy. I detected a glint in her eye as she quickly looked away.

Alana and Terra began to talk about the stew and Alana told Terra that Bull wanted meat in his and had gone to fetch his hatchet. Then she looked at me to see if I had heard her.

I didn't know why Alana was suddenly treating me so unkindly and was so unfair in her assessment of me and I told her so.

"That's what I mean. You are always afraid for your feelings," Alana said. She sneered at me and then pointed off to the right.

I turned to see Bull returning. He was carrying a hatchet. A chill ran through me, which Alana detected with a chuckle. "Be on your guard," she hissed at me.

When Bull arrived she introduced us. "This is Heather, Hugh Farley's heir," she said to Bull. She turned to me. "This is Bull, who was a son to your uncle. You two should have much in common."

I didn't know what Alana meant and I didn't ask. There was a hatchet in Bull's hand and he raised it, fingering the blade with his free hand. I shivered at his gesture. "Hello, Bull," I said finally, trying to make light of my true feeling.

Alana chuckled in the background. I knew I was the brunt of her humor and tried not to let on that I cared. It didn't make sense to me that only a short time had passed since she had talked to me so gently about the matching energies of stick and stones. I thought she might be crazy to suddenly change in a way that endangered me in Bull's presence.

Terra Lenda gave me another quick glance as if to warn me to silence my thoughts, but it was too late.

Alana came toward me and took me aside. "Heather, I thought you were better, that your schizophrenia had lessened its grip on you, but now I see I was mistaken. You are still very much out of control."

I wanted to tell her that I believed that it was her who was out of control, that she was schizophrenic but I managed to keep silent.

"I can't deal with you, Heather," Alana said, eyeing me. She started to turn away then turned back to me again. "Go sit over there," she said, pointing to a rock ledge some twenty feet away, "and work on your stick."

I went to the ledge and sat down to rub the pinkish rock I had found against the stick Alana had given me. While I was aware of the others near the cooking pot, I did not look up until Terra Lenda brought me a dish of stew.

"Submit to the teacher," Terra said, looking me in the eyes as she handed me the dish.

I started to protest that I didn't know what Alana wanted of me but I took the cue from a slight gesture of Terra's hand and remained silent.

Terra returned to Alana and Bull and began to eat and chat lightly with them. I watched the three of them with my peripheral vision, feeling that I was the object of their conversation.

After some time, when the meal was finished, Alana came to me and took the empty bowl from my hands. "If you were Indian," she said in a matter-of-fact tone of voice, "I would bury you up to your neck in the sand and leave you there."

I fidgeted nervously, certain that Alana was misjudging me and yet unwilling to run from her.

She put the bowl on the ground and brought her face close to mine. "Why do you stay, Heather?"

I thought of answering that it was my ranch, and that I was staying to claim my property but I knew that that was not true. After some struggle, I managed to tell Alana that I was staying because I was compelled to be with her. Although there was great argument within myself, I felt I was about to break through some great barrier and I was determined to stick it out.

She backed away a few inches and took a deep breath. "You didn't understand what I was trying to tell you about imagining yourself on thin ice, did you?" she asked.

I thought that she meant that our relationship was on thin ice because she was annoyed with me, and said nothing.

"Do you realize how much abuse you are heaping on me?" she asked.

I wanted to say that it was I who was taking the abuse, that if she were kinder to me that I would respond more favorably, but I remembered that long ago I had used that argument and I recalled how she had mocked me. I lowered my eyes.

"You must leave," Alana said in a gentle voice.

I raised my eyes to meet hers. "I can't leave you," I said.

"Yes, you can. It is the best for you, Heather, and it is the best for me."

CHAPTER 6
DEVELOPING MENTAL POWER

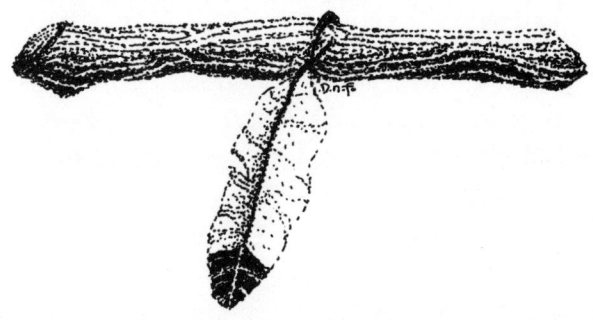

I spent a slow afternoon packing my belongings, preparing to return to my California home. Since the ranch didn't have a phone, I didn't know when I could catch a flight out of Colorado Springs and I didn't worry about it. I decided that I would leave when I was ready and wait for the next available plane when I got to the airport. When I was finally ready to leave and my suitcases were waiting by the front door, I went into the living room and sat down on the couch. Tears streamed down my face as I stared at the empty rocker Alana had sat in the day before and I wondered how so much could change in such a short period of time.

The real reason I had returned to the ranch was because it seemed to be the only real part of my life. It was the part that I used to teach others in my workshops and my books, and, it was the part of my life that gave me a sense of personal fulfillment. As difficult as it was to be with Alana, being with her enriched every aspect of my life. How could I leave? Yet, how could I stay since she had told me to leave?

I rose from the couch, went to the rocker and stood in front of it. Had Alana been seated there now I would have poured my heart out to her and begged her to let me stay, but she was not there. I touched the seat with my hand and turned around to leave. Bull was standing in the doorway.

"Alana sent me. She wants to see you," Bull said eyeing me strangely.

I stared at him, wondering how he could have entered the house without my hearing him.

"She didn't tell me what for. She just said to fetch you," Bull said again.

"You should have knocked," I said bravely, unsure if he was indeed Alana's messenger.

He stared at me as though he felt he did not owe me an answer.

I lowered my eyes and raised them again. "It would have been nice if you had knocked," I repeated.

"I never knocked for Farley," Bull said.

"I'm not Farley," I answered.

"That's for sure, and you've got no claim to his property either," Bull snapped.

I reminded him that he had said that Alana wanted to see me and asked him where I would find her.

"I'll take you," he said.

I hesitated.

Bull grinned. "I wouldn't have to take you anywhere to do you in," he said. "If I wanted to, I could get rid of you right now."

"Bull, I did not ask to inherit my uncle's ranch," I said.

"As good as."

"No, that's not true. I didn't even know my uncle," I explained.

"Alana wants you," Bull said, not acknowledging my statement.

I was hopeful that what he said was true but still hesitated, unsure.

"Well, are you coming or not?"

I decided there was only one way to find out and followed him out the door.

On our way through the meadow, Bull turned to me and asked, "Why is it you make life so difficult for Alana?"

I was unsure of what to say. "I don't do it on purpose," I answered finally.

"But you do it," he said again.

"I do it," I agreed.

We walked on silently for a few moments. Bull took a turn in direction, cutting down the backside of the meadow toward the river instead of continuing up toward the hollow the way I usually went to find Alana. When the river was in view, he stopped.

"See that aspen grove on the other side of the river?" Bull pointed to a small grove of trees a mile or two on the other side.

"Yes," I answered, shading my eyes from the sun with my hands so that I could see better.

"That's where Alana wants you to go. She wants you to meet her there."

"She does?"

Bull turned and glared at me. "That's what I said she said."

I had never been on that part of the property and since it was so far away, I said that I thought I'd better go back and get some supplies from the house.

"She wants you to come now," Bull said. He pointed to the river again. "She's waiting for you over there."

I hesitated, wanting to say something friendly to him, something that would ease the tension between us, so I thanked him for conveying Alana's message to me.

As I set out down the trail to the river I thought of a time when Alana had led me to the river to draw a medicine wheel on the ground. But she had never crossed the river with me. Today, like then, it was a brilliant afternoon. Patches of milk-white clouds accentuated a cobalt blue sky and I thought of how I had prepared to leave the ranch when Bull had appeared in the doorway of the house. A few minutes later and I would have been on my way to the airport. I turned and looked back to see if he was still looking after me, but he had gone.

I stopped at the river's edge and looked across at the aspen grove, which now appeared larger than it had in the distance. I didn't recall seeing it on my previous trips to the river and it struck me how unobservant I had been. It also struck me odd that the river was now high and I had remembered it as low, but then when I had been there before, it had been later in the Summer.

Wondering how to cross, I looked down the river and then up. There was a log jam a short distance up stream and I hurried over to it.

Four or five logs crisscrossed the river bank and beneath them, beavers had built a den out of branches and twigs. I hesitated to see if one of the occupants would stick their head out and then used a corner of the jam to vault myself onto the larger trunk of a tree. The dam shifted in the water under my weight and then sprung back into place. I hurried to the other side.

An animal howled in the distance. I looked in the direction of the sound. It howled again.

Looking into the lonely terrain, I suddenly wished that I had gotten off the ranch before Bull had found me. I knew I didn't belong there, even if it was my ranch. I was out of place. By Alana's treatment of me, she had shown me that I wasn't welcome. She had been harder on me this visit than she had ever been. And, while some of her treatment I believed justified, there was some that seemed unfair. It was difficult enough to perform and speak as Alana wanted. I could not be expected to control every thought as she wished as well.

I paused to look back at the rushing river, noting the sudden change in myself, how i had wanted to stay with Alana before Bull had come to fetch me and how resentful I felt now. Was that what Alana meant when she called me schizophrenic?

There was another howl, a little closer this time and I looked to the right of the aspens, thinking that I might see a wolf, but instead I saw Terra Lenda signaling me with a wave of her arm. I waved back and started to hurry toward her when suddenly she disappeared.

When I reached the place where I had seen her, I looked all around and called out to her, but there was no answer. I considered too, that Bull may be trying to trick me.

There was another howl and then another. I stood frozen to my spot, listening. I was not ten feet from the aspen grove. The cliffs were close to my right. Either the sound came from the tall meadow grasses, the cliffs or from the grove. I remembered what Terra Lenda had told me about herself, that she was a shape shifter, that she came and went according to the imaginings of others, and I wondered if I really had seen her or if she had been a reflection of my imagination. Again I heard a howl, but this time it seemed a long way off.

I stepped between the aspens. To my surprise, Alana was sitting on a fallen tree rubbing a stone against my protection stick. The eagle feather was still tied to its center. She raised her head to look at me and held out the instruments to me. "You left your protection stick," she said. "I wanted you to have it with you."

"Thank you," I said, taking the stick from her, holding it in one hand and the rock in the other.

"I have been hard on you," Alana said, "because it is my job to be hard on you."

"I know that," I said, nodding that I understood. The conflict that I had felt moments before suddenly dissolved.

She studied me as though she had noticed the change.

As always, I was affected by her attention toward me. "I seem to have little control over my mind when you are hard on me," I confessed. "I immediately think angry words at you."

"It is because you have not understood how to control your mind. You still allow it to control you." Alana motioned that I sit on a log across from her. I followed her gaze up, into the grey bark of the tree trunks, to the delicate green foliage at the top. The sun cascaded through the leaves making them seem like finely cut pieces of stained glass. The patterns of light and shadow settled on top of us. She looked at me again. "It is why I asked you to meet me here," she said. "You must learn to control your mind."

"I'll do anything you ask," I said, touching the eagle feather at the center of my stick.

"That's what you say, but your DO says differently."

I lowered my eyes and raised them again. "I always try," I said sincerely.

She shook her head. "Maybe that's the problem. You try too much."

I didn't know what to say. I was aware of the laws of life, that if one tries too hard at something, the results are almost certain failure. There had to be a certain relaxed deflection for an action to produce wanted results. I also realized how very much I wanted to succeed as Alana's apprentice and that my desire for it was getting in the way.

Alana rose from her seat. "I need some help with the horses," she said.

I couldn't imagine Alana needing any help with anything but I jumped to my feet. She turned to glare at me as I trotted after her. After a moment, she asked, "How is the horse I gave you?"

She was asking about Spirit, the young stallion I had taken back to California with me. "He's big," I answered, "and a handful."

"What do you mean?"

I told her how his hormones had been rushing and that everyone wanted me to geld him but that one of his testicles hadn't dropped.

"Do you work him?" she asked.

I answered that I tried but that lately he was too much for me to handle.

"Seems to be the story of your life," she retorted.

I then began to tell Alana how well he had been trained when I had boarded him in a pasture with other young horses. It was only now that I moved him that he began acting up again.

She cast a sideways glance and made a popping noise with her mouth. "He was happy, so he let you make a pet out of him," she said, "but that doesn't mean you trained him. It's like you, I don't have a hold on you. You're respectful when you think I'm nice. It's not the same thing as being trained."

I was annoyed at being compared to a horse but I let it pass.

Alana made a sharp right turn and disappeared behind a protrusion of rock. When I caught up with her she was approaching a small herd of horses in the center of a round clearing. She turned back and glared at me.

I stopped and waited for her to tell me what she wanted me to do.

She motioned me to her. "Do you know why I appear displeased with you?" Alana asked.

"No," I answered.

"Because every time I say something to you, you mentally complain about it. How do you think that makes me feel? Or can't you think about anyone's feelings but your own."

It was uncanny how she knew my every thought. I felt trapped and wished that I was on the airplane, on my way back home to California, when she shrieked at me. "Heather, I asked you a question!"

Unnerved, I started to shake. The horses paused in their grazing to look at me and then continued to eat. It was as though I bothered them but anything Alana did or said was okay.

"You idiot!" she yelled.

I lowered my eyes in an effort to control myself. Never in my association with anyone had I been called such a name.

"Look at me!" Alana demanded, standing in front of me.

I managed to look at her.

"Now smile," she said.

I hesitated, trying to suppress the hate that rose in me and, frightened by it, I finally managed to force a smile.

"Put the smile in your eyes as well," Alana demanded.

I wanted to shout that she was crazy, to tell her to leave me alone; that I didn't need to take such abuse, but I managed to hold my tongue. Deep inside, beneath my emotional tug-of-war, I knew that Alana was deliberately trying to draw an adverse reaction from me and the irony between my hate and love for her made me genuinely smile.

She relaxed and smiled back. "Good," she said, lightly touching me on the arm, "now we can continue." She turned and went over to the stallion Stony and ran her hand down his injured leg. "He'll never be the same," she said. After a moment, she turned to me. Stony looked at me as well. "After something major happens in our lives, we are never the same," she said.

I thought she was referring to what had just transpired between us and so I didn't say anything.

"Hold Stony's mane to steady him while I lift his hoof," Alana said.

I reached up and took hold of a clump of hair in the center of Stony's mane and ran my other hand down his neck, soothing him, then I watched Alana pick up his hoof to examine it. Suddenly Stony flinched. I believed he was about to shift his weight and bump into Alana and so I quickly stepped in front of his chest to protect her.

Alana dropped his hoof. "You stupid bitch!" she yelled.

I moved away from the horse, too astounded to speak.

Alana stepped in front of me, smiling. "Quick! Smile at me," she instructed.

I managed a weak smile.

"Now tell me you love me," Alana said.

"I love you," I managed to say.

She gave me a hug, then turned and slowly began walking away. I watched after her. She stopped and looked back, a hint of a smile on her lips. "Well, come on," she said.

I hurried to catch up.

"Mind control," she began, "comes about when you are so centered within yourself that you no longer worry about having hurt feelings. Do you understand me, Heather?" She paused to look at me.

I nodded, realizing that she had not been in danger when working with the stallion, that she had been in control all the time.

"That doesn't mean that you shouldn't be considerate of other people's feelings, that because you are to be in control of your own, that you insist on that control for others." She paused. Her expression was firm but not unkind. "You must always be kind to others, Heather."

I nodded and looked away.

"You think me unkind to you?" Alana asked.

"I think you are training me," I answered.

"What is different about my harshness to you and someone else's?" she asked.

"Your intent," I answered. "You are doing it for me, not for yourself."

Alana drew in a long, deep breath. I knew she was pleased by what I said. "Tell me what you feel about your training with me?" Alana asked.

I considered what to say, aware that there was no argument within myself, and I told Alana that. I also told her that I felt like someone who had experienced an electric shock, using the analogy of touching the hot wire fence around my horse's corral and how one avoids the wire afterwards. As I spoke, I began to realize the manner in which she had trained me.

"I shifted your assemblage point," Alana said, gazing deeply into my eyes. "If I were to call you an idiot right now, it would mean nothing to you." She smiled. "You would walk away saying, "Oh well, I was just called an idiot again. What do I care? Being called names means nothing to me. Is that not true?"

"Yes," I answered, knowing that it was. I also told her that I was amazed at how differently I perceived life. I told her that before I had met her, life seemed more rigid and pre-determined and now

I didn't know what was going to happen next. I explained that even the way my eyes perceived images was vastly different, that there was a greater dimension to things and that even colors seemed brighter.

"That is because you have shed some of your fear," Alana said. "You no longer have to fear being called names or having your feelings hurt because you know it doesn't matter." She paused. "Do you remember the three rules I gave you?"

I recounted to her the three rules that she had given me on a previous visit to the ranch: 1) It doesn't matter, 2) You don't need to understand everything, and 3) Not to be competitive with others. She asked me to explain them. I reiterated that "it doesn't matter" explodes the false concept that we need to make something out of everything. The feeling of needing to "understand everything" is unimportant in maintaining life on a conscious level. And thirdly, if we are to run a race, we run for our own best time, not to compete with another person.

She nodded approvingly and then hurried her pace.

I had been so absorbed in our communication that I hadn't realized that we had walked so far. Alana made a sudden turn and before us was a chestnut mare and her newborn foal in the same alcove where Alana had said it would be born. The foal was wobbly on his legs but determined to remain upright with his mother.

"You are like this foal," Alana said, "not yet strong enough to be on your own, but strong enough to stand next to me."

I looked at her and realized the truth in what she said. In many ways, Alana was a parent to me; a friend and a teacher sometimes, but mostly a parent.

"What are you thinking?" she asked.

I told her.

"It would be easier if I had been your parent," she added. "As it is I have to rip away the parenting that you did have in order to start anew. It is not easy to strip away one's bondage when they believe it to be holy."

I knew what she meant. My resistance was strongest on matters that I believed to be the truth, things that my parents and society drilled in me as right behavior. I realized suddenly how terrible it was for Alana to try to heal infections that I insisted on keeping. "Why do you do it?" I asked, forgetting myself and falling into sympathy with Alana. Almost as soon as the question escaped my lips, I knew what I had asked.

Alana looked me in the face for what seemed a long time. Tears overflowed from her eyes as she gazed at me with love and compassion. "I do it, Heather," she answered in a soft voice, "because I am a medicine woman and you reached out to me for help."

CHAPTER 7

MORE ABOUT COMPANION ENERGY

"Run!" Alana yelled a short distance from where I crawled on my hands and knees picking weeds around the house.

I looked up at her dumbfounded.

"Run!" she yelled again.

I stood up and faced her and looked around to see what I was supposed to be running from.

"Run! Run! Run! Run!" she shrieked.

I became panicky, certain that some horrible unseen force was coming at me.

"No! No! You're going the wrong way!" she yelled again.

I reversed my position and began to run in the opposite

direction. It occurred to me that Bull must have been on the rampage and was out to get even with me for inheriting my uncle's ranch.

"S t o p!" Alana shrieked.

I stopped and turned to face her. She was obviously angry.

"When I tell you to run, you run," she said harshly.

I looked around for the reason but saw nothing. "Why?" I asked.

"If you are my student, you will do what I tell you, when I tell you, without question. Do you understand, Heather?"

I didn't, but I said I did.

Alana turned and walked away.

I spent much of the afternoon on my hands and knees picking the weeds she had asked me to pick, reflecting back to how she had screamed orders at me to run and then screamed at me to stop. I felt an odd sense of elation over it, as though we were playing a game at which I allowed her to be the leader. I found myself chuckling about the submissive role I was playing. After a while I realized Alana was sitting in the rocker on the front porch, watching me.

I looked up at her and smiled as if to say I was still playing the game and didn't mind it a bit.

She scowled at me in such a way that I lowered my head and resumed picking weeds. It seemed to me she could laugh a little. It was I who was picking the weeds and I was making fun out of the game.

"Heather, come up here," Alana snapped.

I rose to my feet, dusted the dirt from my jeans and went to the bottom of the porch steps and looked up at her.

"What is the matter with you?" she asked.

Not knowing what she was referring to, I didn't answer.

"I asked you a question."

"I don't know what to say," I answered.

"Say something," Alana snapped.

"I don't believe anything is the matter with me," I said soberly. I didn't enjoy this part of the game and I wished that she would lighten up.

"Don't say believe," she said.

"Huh?"

"You are always saying that you believe this and that. Don't say *believe* anymore."

"What should I say?" I asked.

"You're a writer, Heather. Your vocabulary can't be that limited. Say you *think*. At least 'think' denotes some intelligence."

"I believe in things," I argued.

Alana glared at me and I wished that I had kept my mouth shut.

"I'm sorry," I said quickly.

Alana's manner softened. "From now on you believe in nothing, Heather. Instead, you *think*. Okay?"

"Okay," I answered.

She stood up and descended the porch steps, then told me to show her how I picked weeds.

I led Alana to the side of the house where I had been working and dropped to my knees. I reached for a clump of rag grass growing against the house and yanked at it.

"Stop!" Alana commanded.

I stopped and looked up at her.

"You are being careless in pulling that weed and it doesn't want you to pull it," Alana said.

"Huh?" I said dumbly.

Alana glared at me. "Do you know what it is that makes you stay with me?"

I shook my head.

"Your stupidity binds you to me, Heather," Alana said.

Tears filled my eyes and I looked away.

Alana stooped down next to me and took my hand in hers, then she wrapped my hand gently around the weed. "Tell me when the plant becomes resistant to being pulled."

She guided my hand to give a light tug on the rag weed. It started to give and then it resisted. I told her what I felt.

"Ease up on it now and let it know that it's okay for it to let go," Alana said. "And you don't have to tell it in words. Then remove it."

I released my grip on the plant and looked at it kindly and compassionately, then I pulled it easily from the ground.

"When you are working from companion energy, there is no resistance," Alana said. She let go of my hand and looked deeply into me. "It is what you and I are trying to establish between us. When you understand the principles of companion energy, you will stop resisting me."

"But the plant doesn't understand and it does it anyway," I said, puzzled at why working with the plant would be different.

"Precisely the point I wanted you to see," Alana said.

I looked at her questioningly, thinking to myself that if she were kind to me, compassionate, as I had been to the rag weed, I would be less resistant.

"Your instincts are missing, Heather. You think too much. When I tell you to run, you think 'Alana wants me to run' and then you decide to do it. Instead, when you hear run, you should run because your instincts tell you that your teacher would not yell for you to run without good purpose." She stood up and looked down on me. "The plant was more trusting than you. Inwardly, you told it it was okay to be pulled and it accepted your okay."

"But I can't go around accepting what other people say as okay for me," I said, sitting on the ground and looking up at her.

Instead of asking why, Alana said, "I don't know what makes

you the way you are."

"I'll tell you," I said defensively. "There was a time when someone assured me it was okay to borrow a lot of money for a business venture. Well, I did it. When things went wrong, they walked out and left me owing the debt. It took me years to pay that money back."

"We're not discussing that person's role in your life," she said, eyeing me. "We are discussing the way you misbehave with your teacher."

"I've had teachers in my life who have abused me," I asserted, recalling the nuns in Catholic school and how they used to beat me with a ruler for my left-handedness.

"For some, *giving in* wouldn't mean the situation had to turn out badly, but I can see that for you *giving in*, cannot work," Alana said.

"What do you mean?" I asked.

"It's not your nature to give in."

I looked at her with a feeling of regret, as though she had denied me something that I wanted to be. I fought back the tears. "If it's not my nature," I managed to ask, "then why does your telling me that I cannot give in to you hurt so much?"

"Everything hurts you," Alana said brusquely. "I've never known anyone to be so hurt by everything."

Several weeks later Alana invited me onto the porch to play the Stone Game with her. The game is played with eleven stones, which she spread out on the round table in front of her rocker. As the game is played, I was to not pick up the stone that she did not want me to pick up. She chose a stone, then I followed and so on. If played properly, the last remaining stone would be the one she had chosen for me not to pick up. When it was my turn to pick the stone that was "it" I found myself hoping that she would pick it and thereby lose the game.

"I can't play with your anger," she said, looking up at me as she had wrongly chosen the stone I did not want her to pick up on the second round. "You want to be competitive with me, to show me up, and that is not how this game is played. Heather, this is a game to develop companion energy, not competitive energy. Do you understand me?"

Ashamed, I nodded that I did.

Alana rose from her seat and started to leave.

"Alana, I want to clear the air," I said nervously, realizing what I had done.

She glared at me and stomped her feet on the porch. "Clearing the air requires the energy of two people. It is negative. Clearing the air is not living in forward motion. Can you see how negative you are in the things you want to do?"

I felt that I would become sick and looked away.

"Answer me!"

I told her how I felt.

"Acceptance heals, rejection makes sick," she said firmly. "If you are sick, it is because you reject what it is that I am telling you. You are at war with the truth I give you." She hesitated to study me. "A non-resistant person can have a bucket of red paint spilled on them and they will say, "Gee, I wanted to be red today." Do you understand, Heather?"

I nodded, although I wasn't sure I did.

"When you compete with or against somebody, unity is destroyed. ESP demands unity. ESP is companion energy. That is what the Stone Game is about, companion energy or ESP. The conscious mind has to step out before ESP can happen. ESP is as fast as the speed of light.

"Perhaps if you would explain the game as choosing the stone you want chosen rather than not choosing the stone, my mind wouldn't rebel so much," I said in an earnest tone of voice.

"ESP lives in a mirror. It is backwards," Alana said.

I tried rephrasing my point. "Wouldn't it be easier if I picked a stone that I thought you would like me to pick?" I asked.

"Heather, pick a stone because you like it. For ESP to happen, nothing must happen." Alana narrowed her eyes, looking at me. "Okay?"

"Okay," I answered.

Alana sat back down.

This time I picked a stone that I liked and inwardly noted that it was the stone I did not want her to pick up. We played the game perfectly. The last stone left was the one that I had chosen. Alana then silently picked a stone to see if I would cooperate with her. The outcome of the game was to her satisfaction.

"Good," Alana said, pleased that the final stone was the one she had chosen for me not to pick up. "At last there is companion energy working between us."

"You mean, ESP?" I asked.

"ESP is companion energy," Alana said.

For a moment I was overcome with a new understanding of what ESP or extra sensory perception was. I told her what I suddenly understood.

Alana smiled and let out a sigh of relief. She rose from her seat. "And now I want you to take me into town. There is something I want you to do there."

My clothes were very dirty from kneeling on the ground picking weeds and I suggested that I make a quick change into some clean jeans.

"Don't bother," Alana said, "you're fine to go as you are."

When we got into town, Alana asked me to pull up in front of the trading post, which I did and then I followed her inside. She led me to a small picture of an eagle, a hologram hanging over the cash register. It was obviously an inexpensive picture in a cheap, thin black frame, but the eagle pictured in it stood in striking pose, as if in total control of the world around it. I liked it immediately.

Alana watched me looking at the picture and then she asked, "Do you know why you like it, Heather?"

"Because it is my power animal," I answered.

"It is your power animal because it is you," she added.

I looked at her and then back to the picture. Never had I seen an eagle posed so expressively. The strength coming from it totally captivated my attention.

"You look just like it," Alana said, looking at the picture and then at me.

I smiled at her approval.

"Many times I see you standing like that," Alana added. "It is a sign of the strong spiritual warrior in you."

"Thank you," I said, still staring at the picture. "I like it very, very much."

"Then you must buy it," Alana said.

I looked at Alana and then back at the picture. It was obviously an item that was not for sale. One could tell that by the way it was hung off by itself, away from the other merchandise.

"Buy it," Alana repeated.

"I don't think it's for sale," I said softly, "but I'll ask."

I went over to the proprietor who was arranging some jewelry in a case further down the counter and told him how much I liked the eagle picture.

"Just a cheap picture," he said, not looking up.

"I'd like to buy it," I said.

The man looked up from his work. I could see that he was of native American heritage. "My son gave that to me," he said, "and so I couldn't sell it."

I looked at Alana who called me over to her. "I'll wait in the Jeep for you while you buy the picture," she said.

"But Alana," I said quietly, "his son gave him the picture and he says he can't sell it."

"You will find a way," she said and walked out.

I stood in front of the eagle, admiring it.

"It's just a cheap hologram," the proprietor said, noting my continued interest. "It has no value, except to me. My son gave it to me."

"I've never seen an eagle that I've liked so much," I answered in a loud voice.

"Just a cheap print," he said again.

"I'd really appreciate it if you'd sell it to me."

"Can't."

I remained in front of the eagle print admiring it. After awhile, I said, "I'll give you fifty dollars for it."

The man looked up from the display of jewelry he was arranging. "That's too much money for that print," he said.

"I'll give you twenty-five for it."

The man stopped what he was doing and walked over to where I stood looking at the picture. He lifted the frame from the wall and put it down on the counter facing me. "It's just a cheap picture," he repeated. "My son gave it to me so it shouldn't be sold."

"It would mean a whole lot more to me than just a cheap picture," I said, "a whole lot more." I quickly reached in my pocket and took out twenty-five dollars and laid the money on the counter. "It will mean more to me than I can ever tell you."

The man picked up the money. "It's not worth twenty-five

dollars," he said.

"It is to me," I answered, taking it off the counter and holding it next to my chest. "Thank you very, very much." Then I turned and hurried out of the store before the proprietor could change his mind.

Alana was sitting in the Jeep. She turned and grinned at me when I got in with the picture in my hand. Then she asked me to tell her the details of how I got it.

"I told you it was your picture," Alana said when I had finished my story. "The man was Indian and he knew you had to have it. That's why he let you offer him less money and sold it to you."

"Did he know it was my power animal?" I asked.

"In a way he did," Alana said thoughtfully. "His instincts recognized that you were the eagle even if he didn't know it in his mind."

I thought I understood and I told Alana so.

"From now on," Alana said, smiling at me, "I am going to call you by your name." She hesitated as if making sure she had my full attention. "You are now the woman called Winged Wolf."

CHAPTER 8
SETTING THINGS RIGHT

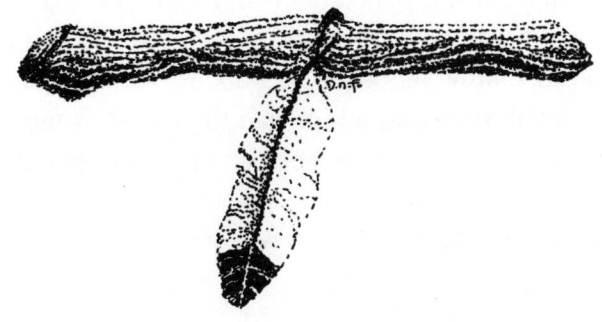

I stood on the other side of Stony while Alana examined his injured leg. This time I did not try to anticipate her moves, or try to protect her when she did not need protecting. I merely stood by patiently waiting and watching as she had instructed me to do. When she had finished she lowered Stony's hoof to the ground and stood up to stroke his long slender, grey neck to the withers where she began to knead her fingers into the short, thick fur. Stony stretched his neck in contentment, his upper lip gracefully dancing to the movement of her fingers on his back.

I giggled at his performance.

Alana turned and peered over his withers at me, the lower part of her face was invisible. Even so, I could tell from her eyes that she was smiling. "Would you like to work Stony?" she asked.

I had thought that the injury to Stony's leg had made him unworkable and so I hesitated.

"He's well enough for simple work," Alana said, "a walk around the hollow. A few halts with left and right turns won't hurt him and I think he'd like it." She stepped away from Stony and left me at his left side.

The grey stallion watched as Alana moved away then turned his head toward me and touched me with the end of his nose.

I stroked his neck then tilted my head forward, imitating a horse's posture when he begins to walk as Alana had taught me. Stony accepted the signal and began to walk with me. When it came time to turn, I tossed my head and shoulder to the side and crossed one leg over the other to exaggerate my movements. Stony followed, shoulder to shoulder, as we turned 180 degrees to head for the other end of the hollow.

"Bring him to a halt," Alana cried.

I brought my head and shoulders up in the exaggerated movement Alana had previously shown me and stopped. Stony stopped next to me.

"Walk!" Alana called.

We began to walk again.

"Stop!"

We stopped.

"Turn right!" she instructed.

We turned right.

"Stop!"

We stopped.

"Turn left!"

We turned left.

"Stop!"

We stopped.

"Step out in front of him and hold your hand up for him to stay, then walk away," Alana instructed.

I did as I was told. Stony stayed behind.

"Call him back to you," Alana said.

I lowered my head and shoulders, bobbing my head as I stepped backward in a slow, dancing motion. Stony arched his neck as if imitating me and pranced toward me.

"Very good!" Alana called out. "Very good! Now leave Stony and come here."

I signaled Stony to stay, then turned and went toward Alana. Stony hesitated, took a few bites of grass and then began to follow me.

Alana chuckled. "You have done well, Winged Wolf," she said, smiling at me.

I smiled back, exalted by her approval and the sound of my new name. I was filled with such bliss that I felt intoxicated.

Stony continued past me, beyond where Alana stood, and began to graze. "See that bay down there, next to the side of the mountain," Alana said, pointing to a horse that was grazing off to our left.

"Yes."

"Go and bring her to me, Winged Wolf," she instructed.

I turned and walked toward the bay. When the horse noticed me, I stopped to let her become accustomed to my presence and then slowly continued toward her again, pausing every once in a while so that she did not become alarmed and run away. Finally, I walked up to her, clucked, hesitated, held out my hand and stroked her face in "hello."

"Go trot!" I said, crisscrossing my hands in front of her face and brushing one up against the other. Alana had previously taught me that such a movement sends a flash of psychic light that the horse can see as a signal to move away. Immediately, the bay turned and began to trot in the opposite direction. After a few moments, she turned to face me again. I lowered my head and shoulders in a swooping motion and took a few steps backwards to signal the bay to me. As she approached, I then stepped forward and raised my body in stop motion. The bay stopped in front of me. I ran my hand down the length of her nose and stepped to her left shoulder, patted it, then lowered my upper body and began to walk forward. The bay followed. I stopped. She stopped. I walked and she walked, until we came face to face with Alana.

Alana motioned me to step away, which I did, then I turned to watch her.

With a twig in hand, Alana tapped the bay on the left knee. The bay bent her leg and then put it down again. She tapped again and this time the bay bent both knees and knelt to the ground. Alana then slowly moved to her side and climbed on top of her. The animal rose to her feet again with Alana on her. She smiled at my surprise.

"Alana, that's wonderful!" I called. Never had I known anyone who had such a rapport with all life. I thought of how Alana had taught me to correctly pull a weed. Seeing how easily the bay obeyed her made me appreciate an even greater sense of companion energy.

Alana stared at me for what seemed a long time. The horse remained absolutely motionless under her. "I want you to find Bull and ask him to change the oil in your Jeep," she said finally.

I was startled by her request and remained silent.

"It must be done right away," Alana said.

I considered how I would ask Bull and quickly decided that I would hire him to do the job.

"If you pay him, Winged Wolf, you will make him your servant, but you will not make him your friend. If you do not pay him, you will make him a hero through his usefulness."

It amazed me how Alana always seemed to know my thoughts. I wondered if she knew how afraid I was of Bull as well.

"Your fear of Bull is rooted in the knowledge that you have about his anger for you," Alana said.

She knew.

"I again caution you because of the anger you are carrying in yourself. Your anger intensifies his." Alana hesitated, her eyes gazed in a broad sweep behind me and then she looked directly at me again. "Winged Wolf, control yourself and you control everyone and everything in your environment."

"Suppose he has a knife? He had one in his hand a couple of weeks ago as he was coming toward the house," I whined.

"Did he try to injure you with it?"

"No, but when I saw him, I became very frightened and ran," I answered.

"There is always junk sitting around somewhere," Alana said. The horse shifted restlessly from foot to foot. "If you don't want it, don't pick it up. Pick up only the good stuff, Winged Wolf."

I was struck by her words, which meant to me that I had placed importance on the knife Bull was carrying without knowing his intent. I nodded that I understood.

"Remember, if you are being controlled by someone or something, it is because you won't let go of them or it," Alana said.

It was true I had been afraid of Bull and I dramatized that fear in me, feeding it. "Thank you," I said, humbled by her wisdom.

"And smile, Winged Wolf," Alana said lightly. "Moving forward spiritually is somber business, but the display of your life should not be somber." Then, with a movement of her knee against the girth of the horse, she signaled the bay to turn around and began to trot the horse across the meadow, leaving me alone.

I watched her go and then turned to start back to the house. Bull was standing behind me. Startled, I hesitated, unsure of how long he had been there or what to say. Then I recalled how, a few moments before, Alana had gazed into the distance behind me. It must have been as Bull was approaching.

"Will you change the oil in the Jeep for me?" I asked politely.

Bull gave me a hard stare and then nodded. "Sure," he said.

"Will you do it now?" I asked.

Bull's eyes narrowed as if he was deeply thinking about my request. "Okay," he said finally, and he turned and led me out of the hollow, down the hill toward the house.

"Tell me about my Uncle Farley," I said, watching as Bull spread a cloth over the Jeep bumper so as not to scratch the paint. He then reached for the dip stick and ran his fingers through the thin, dark oil that clung to it.

"It's dirty," Bull said. "When's the last time you changed it?"

I had believed that Alana merely used changing the Jeep oil as a way of bringing Bull and me together and now I realized that her request had been practical as well. "About eight months," I answered.

"Too long!" Bull shot back, glaring at me. "You gotta take better care of your Jeep."

"I can see that," I replied gratefully and, wanting to apply the hero principle that Alana mentioned, I asked, "Will you take care of it when I'm gone?"

He glared at me again and didn't answer.

"What was my Uncle Farley like?"

"Why didn't you come and find out?"

I hesitated. Bull slipped under the Jeep with a wrench and pan to drain the old oil. "No one in my family ever said much about Hugh Farley," I said. "And when I asked, they never answered me."

Bull stuck his head out from under the Jeep and glared at me again. "Why didn't ya come and check him out for yourself?"

I didn't know what to say. Often, as a young girl, I had been curious about my uncle but, as I got older, I somehow forgot about him. "I grew up in Virginia," I said. "Have you ever been there?"

Bull did not answer.

"There's a saying back East, 'never rock the boat'."

Bull stuck his head out from under the Jeep again. "What's that supposed to mean?"

"In this case, it meant that it was wise for me to keep still while I was living under my parents' roof," I said.

"You been living under your parents' roof all this time?" Bull asked.

"No," I answered, looking away. Bull stuck his head back under the car. He grunted as the bolt holding the oil pan turned free and the oil came rushing out into the extra container. "I just got busy," I went on, "but I knew that one day I'd find out about my uncle."

After a moment Bull crawled out from under the Jeep and rose to his feet. Then he reached for the fresh cans of oil to pour them into the chassis. "Well, I was here all the time. I was never too busy for your uncle. I never left him once in my whole life." He turned and snarled at me as he emptied the last can of oil. "This is my ranch, not yours. Your Jeep is fixed, now why don't you get out of here and leave us alone?"

A part of me wanted to jump into the Jeep and drive off and another part wanted to scream at Bull that I was the owner of the land and it was he who should leave, but I managed to remain silent. I tried to imagine what response Alana would give if she were in my shoes, but no answer came. I knew it was because she would never be in such a situation. I was attracting Bull's feelings by being the person I was. Alana would never acknowledge his negativity. That was it. I would turn the lemons into lemonade by ignoring his anger. "The townspeople seemed to think Hugh Farley was a wonderful man," I said finally.

"He was the best!" Bull looked me full in the face and, for the first time, I saw a gentle quality in him, noticing too that he was a young man, probably in his late twenties, with impish dimples on either side of his cheeks. He had dark, almost black eyes and his thick, short-cropped dark hair cowlicked in all directions. His stocky body did make him appear rather bullish. He reminded me of a cartoon character.

"How old were you when you came to the ranch?" I asked, wanting to know more about him.

Bull's face hardened again. "What d'you want to know for? I live here. I've always lived here and I will always live here. But you won't!" he screamed, shaking his fist.

There was nothing I could say. Recalling that Alana had warned me not to be a part of someone else's anger, I turned and walked toward the house. He was still yelling as I opened the door and went inside, bolting it shut behind me.

A short time later there was a knock at the door. I looked out to see who it was and saw Bull and Terra Lenda standing there. I slid back the dead bolt and opened the door.

"Bull's a bully," Bull said. His expression reminded me of an apologetic little boy. He had tears in his eyes. "I was afraid you were going to tell me that I couldn't live here anymore."

I looked from Bull to Terra Lenda to Bull again. "I would never do that," I said, then I looked away. I knew that I was capable of becoming angry enough to ask him to leave.

"You really would, wouldn't you?" Bull asked.

"I have thought of it," I answered, "but I don't really want you to leave."

"Then why did you think of it?" Bull nervously looked to Terra Lenda for support, who nodded that he was doing okay.

"I thought of it because there is a selfish part of me and because I don't know you," I replied.

"I'll tell you about myself," Bull said.

I stepped outside and suggested that we sit on the porch to talk. Terra Lenda took the rocker, while Bull and I sat shoulder to shoulder on the steps. I glanced up at Terra for comment but she remained silent.

"I was born here," Bull blurted out. "My mother died when I was two and Farley took care of me."

I noted his intensity as I glanced at the young man's face and chose my question carefully. "Are you related to my uncle?"

Bull shook his head. "He raised me up though."

It occurred to me that Bull was retarded and did not go to school. He seemed to know what I had been thinking.

"Farley taught me how to read some, and write," Bull went on. "He also taught me about the mountains, him and Alana. Mostly I lived with Farley but sometimes I lived with Alana. She took me to the Pacific Ocean once." He turned to face me.

I was astounded since I believed that Alana had never been off the property.

"Alana is a medicine woman, you know," Bull said.

"I know," I replied.

"She's taken me many, many places," Bull said.

"She has?"

"More than you can count on your hands," Bull said.

"Where else did she take you?" I asked.

"She took me to the Lakota reservation, and she took me to the moon."

"To the moon?"

The light danced in Bull's eyes and he nodded his head.

"How did she do that?" I asked. Then, suddenly, flashing on my experience with the eagle, I realized how Bull had traveled with Alana.

"Farley came with us sometimes," Bull went on, "and sometimes I saw my mother. I loved seeing my mother. She died when I was two, but she's even prettier now."

I didn't respond. Instead I asked, "Did Alana ever teach you about the horses?"

Bull's face lit up. "She lets me help her sometimes. I even rode Stony once."

I began to realize that Bull was mentally a child and that his anger toward me had been the reaction of a child afraid of being hurt. He had been defensive because I had been defensive. In his simple state of mind anyone or anything new was a threat. And when I had been fearful of him, distrusting him, he assumed my feelings for his own, magnifying them. He had shown me the negative side to companion energy by reflecting my negative feelings.

"Bull," I asked seriously, "why do you think my uncle left me the ranch?"

Bull turned his head to look at me. "Because he wanted you to come. He talked about you all the time. Heather this, Heather that. He always wanted you to come to the ranch and you never did."

"Why didn't he write to me?"

"That wasn't his way. He wanted you to come and you never did."

"I would have if I had known."

"Couldn't you hear him calling you? He talked about you all the time."

I looked away from the young man's face and stared into the mountains. There had been times when I had thought of Uncle Farley, many times, and times that I had dreamed of him as well. But it never occurred to me that he had been calling me. Did he leave me the ranch to make sure I would come?

"If only I had known," I said regretfully. I reached into my jean pocket and pulled out an oblong stone worn smooth from handling and I held it in the palm of my hand to show Bull. "This is a lodestone that Uncle Farley gave to me when I was nine. It was the only time he visited me. When he gave me the stone, he said that its magnetic quality would keep the connection between us. I've carried it all these years."

"Why didn't you come?" Bull asked, gazing at the stone in my hand.

Tears came into my eyes and I shook my head. "I don't know," I said. "I just didn't, but I wish I had."

"It's too late now," Bull said.

"Why did he leave me the ranch?"

"To make you come here," Bull answered.

I looked at Bull, then at the vast terrain. It was the most beautiful place I had ever seen. Every color of wildflower covered the meadows. The mountains towered in every direction. There was abundance in everything. I thought of Alana, the horses, my experience with the eagle, and all that I had learned. Life was impeccable here, as well as gorgeous. My uncle had wanted me to come so that I could experience it and so that I could learn.

I closed my hand about the lodestone and touched Bull lightly on the cheek. "Thank you for helping me," I said, "for being a friend." Then I turned to Terra Lenda to thank her as well, but she was gone.

I spent the next couple of days alone, thinking about my Uncle Farley and his reason for giving me the ranch. Now that his purpose was accomplished, it didn't seem right that I should remain the owner. Bull's whole life had been spent nurturing the ranch and the land with my uncle and the others. While I would always feel welcome there, by all rights, I knew it belonged to him.

Comfortable with my resolve, I drove into town and stopped at the bank. I went inside and asked the manager for a Quit Claim and with him as a witness, I relinquished my claim to Farley's Ranch and signed it over to Bull. I told the manager that, if for any reason Bull should require money to keep it, such as money for taxes, I would take care of it. Then I left my name and California address, asking the manager to contact me if any necessity arose. Finally, with a copy of the deed transfer in hand, I returned to the ranch.

Alana and Bull were at the corral behind the house. Bull was repairing the board fence, nailing it fast while Alana looked on. A feeling of deja vu swept over me and I was reminded of the days when Alana and I had used the corral to train Spirit, the horse she had given me. I waved in greeting.

Alana waved back then returned her attention to what Bull was doing, showing him that extra support should be added to the area he was repairing since it was an area where an animal had pushed through while in confinement. "Always brace a vulnerable spot," Alana explained, glancing up at me as she spoke, "and you will know a vulnerable spot by its weakness." She looked back to Bull who was adding an extra short piece of board to the broken spot.

Finally Alana acknowledged me again. "Well, Winged Wolf, is there anything new in town?" she asked.

"Yes," I said, handing her the documents that transferred the property deed into Bull's name.

Alana studied the document for what seemed a long time

before she looked up at me again, then she walked me away from Bull, to the other end of the corral, and asked, "Why did you do this?"

I told her of my conversation with Bull and explained to her the conclusion I had reached. I added, "Not having my name on the deed merely changes the attitude that I carried about myself as the landowner. Yet it will always be my land, just as it is your land. To me, the deed is really unimportant; but to Bull," I motioned to the document in Alana's hands, "this deed means everything."

Alana smiled approvingly. "Go and give it to him, Winged Wolf," she said.

As I took the documents from Alana's hands, I looked into her eyes. There was a light glowing in them, a glow of tenderness, respect and love, which seemed to reach out and touch the deepest part of me. I could barely breathe. A sudden ecstatic rapture took control of me and I raised my hand and held it tightly against my chest. I could feel the vibrations of a melody as though my heart was singing. I let out a gasp of delight. For a moment more, Alana continued to gaze into me, then she turned and walked away.

CHAPTER 9

THE TRUTH ABOUT HIGHER CONSCIOUSNESS

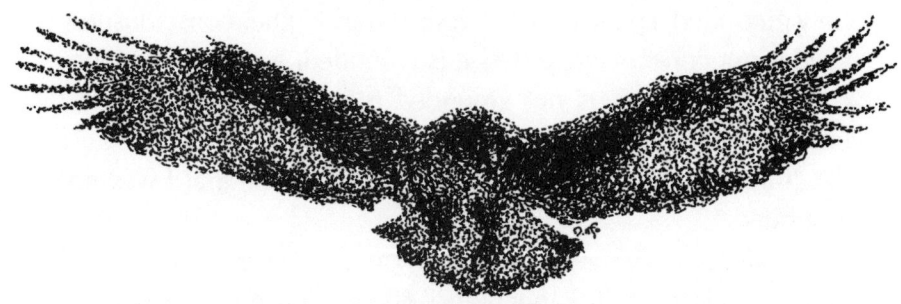

"**I** want to talk to you about schizophrenia," Alana said, as I finished straightening the bed I had made for myself inside of her cave. She went outside the cave and sat down on a rock outside the entrance to wait for me.

I went outside and sat on the ground opposite her. As I waited for her to speak, I tied my hair back, away from my face.

Alana watched me. "Living in nature seems to agree with you, Winged Wolf," she said.

I told Alana that I had never been more happy in my life, then I giggled, explaining to her what I believed the reactions of my friends would be to giving away the ranch and taking up residency in my medicine teacher's cave in the hills instead of staying in the ranch house with Bull.

Alana smiled. "It pleases me that you are so happy," she said, "but now we must get down to business."

I stopped fidgeting and became still, noting how rapturous I felt in her presence. I hoped to stay with her forever.

"Winged Wolf, I want you to know that there are people who have a higher consciousness than Alana," she began.

When Alana spoke of herself by name I found myself paying particular attention.

"It is not the height of one's consciousness that is important, but how grounded a person's consciousness is. Higher consciousness itself is not constructive unless it is grounded. A person of higher consciousness who is not grounded is schizophrenic. Do you understand me, Winged Wolf?"

"I think so," I answered. "You used to tell me that I was not grounded."

"That's true, Winged Wolf. When I met you, you had your head in the clouds, living in other planes of consciousness, unaware of your true physical circumstances." Alana paused, eyeing me. "When we first met, I was very worried. Before your uncle died, he asked me to work with you and I said I would, but when I met you I didn't think it would work between us. Here you were, already a woman of higher consciousness, perhaps even higher than myself, but because of your lack of grounding, your worldly self was completely schizophrenic." Alana rose from her seat, stretched and sat back down again. "The schizophrenic state," she continued, "is all seeing, all knowing with no DO." She stopped and looked at me, then added, "Are you taken with the idea that you could have a higher consciousness than myself?"

I was embarrassed that she knew what I had been thinking and remained silent. Alana then proceeded to remind me how I used to use my identity with the world to find fault with her, as well as to try and make her small by sociologically comparing her to what I considered normal. "Finally," she said, "you learned to quit trying, that I had no bottom." She explained that whereas the knowledge of a schizophrenic is gained by short circuit, without life experience, she was able to live everything she knew. She was able to live her consciousness. "The schizophrenic is filled with knowledge gained off the path. They are the watchers, and not being in the film causes them no change.

"Listen carefully, Winged Wolf. If you live your life as one watching a film, your timing gets wrong. Bad timing makes life difficult. It makes one feel like life is forever passing them by or that they are out of synchronization with the rest of the world. Such a person tends to think that she is better than most people and she tends to be very critical of others." Alana paused, studying me. "Are you following me, Winged Wolf?"

"I think so," I answered again.

"For instance," Alana went on, "your training with me would have been easy if you had already experienced all the knowledge you had previously acquired."

"When we first met, you said that I already knew everything but wasn't free to express it," I reiterated. "Is that what you meant?"

"Yes, Winged Wolf. That is what I meant." Alana rose from her seat again. "Now, let's take a walk."

I got up from the grass.

"Bring your protection stick with you," Alana instructed.

I ducked inside the cave and picked up my protection stick from a ledge near the entrance. I was smoothing my eagle's feather when I came back outside.

Alana eyed me from head to toe and then began walking. I trotted a few steps to catch up with her.

"People have to learn to stop communicating with television and books and instead, look their compadres in the eye, soul to soul," Alana went on.

"But what do you do when someone abuses that communication, when they take advantage of you?" I asked.

"Practice silence, Winged Wolf," Alana answered, turning her head to look at me. "Silence is a shield to create proper energy to make balance when someone steps on your toes."

We walked on silently for a time. I was thinking about what Alana had said in conjunction with other people I knew, comparing my life with theirs. Out of the blue, she told me that I "must stop identifying with the walk of others."

We walked on silently for a time and then I asked Alana if higher consciousness wasn't in itself a form of protection.

"It is," Alana agreed, "if we stay on our path. Nothing can harm us as long as we stay on our path."

I wasn't sure I understood what she meant by path. I asked her if path meant belief system.

Alana shook her head. "I already told you I don't want you believing anything. To use belief as a path would stifle the creative spirit in you. Being true to your path means being true to yourself, by thinking, speaking and acting from your true self, not the self that you believe you should be or the self that others believe you to be."

"You mean I will never again be afraid as long as I stay on my path?" I asked.

"It doesn't matter." Alana gave me a sideways glance and then explained. "Fear in itself is not bad," she said. "Used properly it is a signal, like pain, which tells us there is something more than meets the eye. Fear can be put to work by making us stay on top of a situation, by paying attention, which equals the other end of the stick."

I looked at my stick, hoping she would elaborate but she went on. "Instinct equals knowing, and knowing equals higher consciousness but," she paused long enough to make sure I was following her in thought, "knowing does not equal instinct." She paused again to motion to a doe and her fawn grazing nearby. "The animals teach us. By their instincts, they can guide our consciousness, guide us to our inner voice. The nature of a grounded, well-balanced person with higher consciousness is to be alive to the nature of their own instincts, as well as the instinctual nature of all life. The presence of a particular animal becomes a sign just like a black cloud signals us that there is rain overhead. Each animal has a strength and each animal has a weakness. For instance, the presence of deer can alert us to a quiet reserve of inner strength. The fact that the deer do not run from us means that the strength is ours.

I interjected that I had always believed instinct to be on the physical level of consciousness and therefore part of the lower, rather than higher consciousness of life.

Alana glared at me and then shook her head. "Instinct is connected to higher consciousness through experience. Higher consciousness that exists without instinct is imbalanced. If instinct isn't developed, a schizophrenic personality, meaning the personality of a confused person, takes over. If the conscious brain is not running on instinct and not in tune with the inner voice, then the DO of a person will have mistakes in it.

"Instinct is a part of the inner voice, although the inner voice isn't always instinctual and that's a danger. The inner voice can make life seem like a dream if it isn't connected to instinct. When a person feels that life is dreamlike, it is because their instinct is not present. Do you understand me?" She stopped walking and turned to face me.

I hesitated to consider her words. Many times I had had the

feeling that I had been living in a dream.

Alana asked what I was thinking.

I told her that I was reflecting on what she had said.

"Don't reflect," Alana snapped. "Reflection is looking at the mirror images of things. Instead stay with me. Pay attention to what I am saying to you NOW."

"Okay."

Alana picked up where she left off and began walking again. She spoke very slowly so that I did not have to struggle to keep up in thought. "Animals are our link to higher consciousness. They are our energy sources to develop our instincts. Learning from animals keeps us from continuing to run after the power is turned off."

"Huh?"

"You don't know what I mean?"

"No."

"Have you ever turned off the motor in a car and had it cough and then start to run with the key turned off?"

"I think they call it *dieseling*," I said, "but I still don't understand what you mean."

"Animals live in the NOW," Alana said, "and so when they stop an activity, their minds don't mull over things. When most people do things they are still thinking about it long after they're finished. In other words, they continue to run after the power is turned off."

I started to question her further but didn't get the chance.

"But that's enough," Alana said, rounding a corner. "Today I want to teach you about shape-shifting. Although you have had some experiences with it, it will be a new chapter in your education." She paused. "Ah, Terra Lenda is here to help us."

I looked up to see Terra Lenda standing not more than ten feet in front from us. I wondered how she could have come so unnoticed, but I was becoming used to it. Her appearances and disappearances had been a mystery to me for some time.

Alana embraced Terra and then turned to look around at the nearby cliffs. "What are the signs?" she asked Terra.

"I have seen both eagles and hawks flying today, and a falcon." Terra Lenda answered.

Alana looked up to the skies. There was not a bird in flight. Then she began to study the cliffs, asking that I do the same and for me to tell her what I saw.

I told her that I didn't see anything, that all of the winged creatures seemed to have left the area or that they were hiding.

"It is because you are here," Alana replied. "They are not sure that you are ready for adoption."

Terra nudged me from behind and whispered, "You are ready." Then in a louder voice, she added, "The wolf will fly today."

I couldn't imagine what she was talking about so I kept quiet.

Alana pointed to a ledge on the side of the cliff several hundred feet above us. "It will be a good place, but not easy to reach by foot." she said

"Let her fly up there from here," Terra said.

Alana shook her head. "She'd never be able to take off from the ground and fly up."

I began to realize that they were talking about me, as though they planned for me to fly like a bird.

"No," Alana added thoughtfully, "she is going to climb to that ledge to make her flight."

"Are you talking about me?" I asked.

"Yes, Winged Wolf," Alana answered. "I am talking to Terra about you climbing to that ledge," she pointed overhead, "and flying from it, like a fledgling learning to fly from a tree branch."

"You can't be serious," I said nervously.

"She is serious," Terra added, chuckling. She nudged me again and, as I turned to face her, a hawk flew past and she suddenly disappeared.

I looked around to find her.

Alana pointed up, to the ledge on the side of the cliff. There Terra Lenda sat with her feet dangling over the edge.

I remembered the hawk flying past her face and was afraid to ask how she had gotten up there.

"It's amazing that you have no questions," Alana said, annoyed at my silence. "If ever there was a time for you to ask them, it is now."

"Alana, I don't know what to say," I answered.

"Then don't say anything, but rather ask what you do not understand."

I was dumbfounded and could not speak.

"Winged Wolf, always you ask me questions when I wish you to remain silent, and now, you remain silent when I wish you to ask me questions. Be kind to me," Alana said mockingly.

Terra waved from the cliff.

All the muscles in my body seemed to tighten and a tremor rippled through me. I knew Alana was watching me but I couldn't control my nervousness.

"Get on your hands and knees," Alana suddenly barked.

I got down on my hands and knees.

"Now pick the weed growing under your chest in the way that I have taught you, and give it to me."

I struggled for control and managed to look down at the ground. Just beneath me was a small clump of chickweed. I carefully placed my fingers around the stem at the base of the root and silently asked the plant to give itself to me. I pulled it gently and easily from the ground and handed it up to Alana.

"You may stand up now," Alana said in a gentle voice.

I rose to my feet, feeling much better. Terra Lenda was standing next to Alana. Both medicine women were looking at me. I glanced up to the ledge on the side of the cliff to be sure Terra was here and not there. Terra Lenda began to giggle.

"Are you all right now, Winged Wolf?" Alana asked.

"Yes," I answered, amazed at how much better I felt. I knew Alana had had me pick the weed to re-ground myself so that I could continue in companion energy with her.

"I want you to do everything I do. Okay?" Alana instructed.

"Okay," I answered.

She began to laugh. It wasn't a fake laugh but deep-bellied, full blown laughter. After a time of watching her, I began to laugh at her laughing and then the laughter became my own. Finally, she stopped. I stopped as well. Terra Lenda clapped her hands as if to say she enjoyed the show.

Alana shook her head. "It took you too long to laugh with me. The delay could have killed you. In order for you to survive you must stay in companion energy with me, which means matching my energy through imitation. And it is very important that you do exactly as I do, without hesitation. Do you understand me, Winged Wolf?" Alana looked deeply into me as she spoke, which made me feel both attentive and ecstatic.

"Yes," I answered, aware of the seriousness of her request and the possible consequences if I failed. "I will do my best."

"Let's hope your best is good enough," Alana added.

"I will do as you say and do as you do," I answered, rephrasing my affirmation.

Alana turned to look at Terra Lenda. I did the same.

Terra seemed to be enjoying the attention because she immediately began to flutter as though excited.

"Look at Terra from your soft vision," Alana instructed.

I shifted my eyes off focus and looked at the periphery around Terra as well as Terra herself. Gradually I began to notice that the excited flutter that I had sensed in Terra was more than an emotional response. Her whole countenance actually twittered or fluttered as though she were a bird a split second before taking to flight. I was so amazed that I turned and looked directly at Alana.

"No! No, Winged Wolf. You must not look at me," Alana scolded. "If you are functioning in companion energy with me, you are looking at what I am looking at and in the same way. When you turn to face me, you break that bond of energy-matching between us and you are not yet ready to stand on your own. In other circumstances, you could have been killed."

I turned and looked back at Terra again but she was no longer fluttering in the same way. The corners of her mouth were turned down as if to say that I messed up, but that it was okay, that we would try again when I was ready.

Suddenly Alana yelled, "Run, Winged Wolf!"

Alana had taught me to run in the direction I was facing when she asked me to run. This time Terra Lenda was directly in front of me and I hesitated, then ran around her.

"No. No. Stop!" Alana shouted.

I stopped and turned around to face her.

I explained that I would have run into Terra Lenda if I had not run around her.

Alana glared at me and then turned and walked away.

I hesitated, not knowing what to do.

Terra Lenda nudged me from behind. "Maintain your energy with her," she whispered.

I hurried after Alana but said nothing when I caught up with her. We walked on silently for a time. I noticed with some pleasure that as Alana's left foot came down and touched the ground, mine did as well. We were walking in unison. Even the motion of our arms swung in the same direction at the same time. The only difference between us was that I carried my stick in my right hand and Alana did not have a stick. Suddenly, Alana stopped, reached to the ground with her left hand, picked up a rock and hurled it ahead of us. I did the same. She began to run and I ran. She skipped. I skipped. She stopped and I stopped. Ahead of us was a cliff wall and she began to run. I ran with her. We seemed to step into the wall, twirl around and come out of it again. Afterward, Alana spoke to me. "What do you think just happened?" she asked.

I told her that I did not know exactly, that it seemed that our vibrations intensified to make it appear that we had walked into the cliff.

"No, Winged Wolf," she said, shaking her head. "It was not a trick. We did step inside of the cliff."

I asked how that was possible, saying that the material world had a certain solidity to it that was impenetrable.

"It is time I talked to you about energy," Alana said.

We sat down on the grass facing each other. I put my protection stick between us so that I would not fidget with it while she spoke.

"Pay attention, Winged Wolf," Alana began. "Even if what I am about to tell you does not make sense, follow me word for word. Leave your questions alone until I am finished. Okay?"

"Okay," I answered.

"Energy is movement. All matter moves. Energy has two elements—positive and negative. Wherever these two elements co-exist there is energy." Alana paused to see that I was attentive and then went on. "All life has energy. This means that there are two elements in all life. The heartbeat of the great mystery is nothing more than a little dab of 'all things are connected to all things.' We can feel and know many things about the great mystery but we can never know it all. This fact presents a battle for many seekers, but if we could uncover the great mystery, the discovery would cause the great mystery not to exist, or lose Its purpose and power. For It to stay hidden gives movement to our walk on earth.

"As our inner light grows so does the understanding of infinity. As our understanding of infinity grows so does our understanding that to try to rush to higher learning is a movement that puts us in another part of the chain and that nothing is gained but lost time.

"Lost time is a personal story and a lack of understanding of self in the scheme of the great mystery. If you rush, you lose synchronicity with natural energy and push discovery of self further from your reach. As you climb to enlightenment and reach higher and higher understanding of self, you can gain personal power if the personal story is developed with the heart beat of the unity around you. Unity is where you are—inner and outer. Unity is your permission to accept yourself as sacred as you walk forward."

Alana stopped speaking. She seemed to be looking at something around me as well as my person. Finally, she continued. "We now are ready to touch upon a concept that I want you to understand. I will call it the Energy Story. To understand the concept, let's look at a scene and the energy that is being created. Close your eyes, Winged Wolf."

I did as I was told and closed my eyes.

"Imagine you are in a marketplace with many other people in a country where you do not understand the language. As you walk around, filled with curiosity and wonderment, you become aware of the energy of the marketplace, a vibration that you can feel surrounding you." Alana paused before she went on.

"Did you notice that your imagination started to take over where logic and deduction would be at work if everyone in the marketplace was speaking a language you understood?"

I nodded and said that I did.

"Since you did not understand what anyone was saying, you only felt the energy of what they were saying and of what was happening there. This is a way to seek and understand energy. If you spoke the language, then what you would see and hear would be only the story, without the energy interpretation because of the focus of your logic and deduction at work, instead of imagination. Also your imagination is unlimited if you use soft vision.

"Using soft vision, imagination will float with the scene. If the scene is pleasant, the imagination will have no reason to run with some fantastic yarn, so WHAT YOU ARE, experiences the energy story or the true ecological balance of the scene."

I opened my eyes and looked into Alana's.

"Winged Wolf, if we seek the energy story, instead of merely accepting what the outer story tells us, we develop personal power. The power comes to us because we are truly in the moment and connected with our instincts. Shamans have kin with their energy story and use it at will to lead a story, or a student, or whatever or whoever they wish. This is the direction from which I see life. I teach from personal power. From an individual's energy story, I can see what direction I need to go with my teaching to develop personal power in that student, whether it be a horse or a person. I teach from my perfect self to their perfect self.

"What a person is, is not important, because what they are thinking is based on their personal set of rules, and these get in the way of learning. I empower the perfect self and push out the infection that is causing the block to move forward.

"As long as we use logical deduction we are not in the moment. Instead our perfect self is standing outside. Where logic exists, so does ego. The little self, the Napoleon of order and judgment, has no time to develop true energy for the self to live freely. What I mean by this is our ego is a tool we should use, not a tool that uses us. Ego is a tool that offers a means to evaluate ourselves when we need it. It should never rule our lives. So you see, ego is good if it is used sparingly. This is where the medicine wheel can be put to good use. It is a tool to understand growth and balance. It teaches us to broaden our viewpoints, not just in one or two directions but to reach out in all directions, to encompass the wheel. If instead, we look at only our strong points, the strong gets too strong and causes disease in the ecology of self."

I looked at Alana questioningly. What did her explanation of energy, of the medicine wheel and ego have to do with walking into the cliff?

As though I had spoken aloud, she answered, "It has everything to do with walking into a cliff, and nothing at all."

CHAPTER 10
EXPERIENCES WITH THE ANIMALS

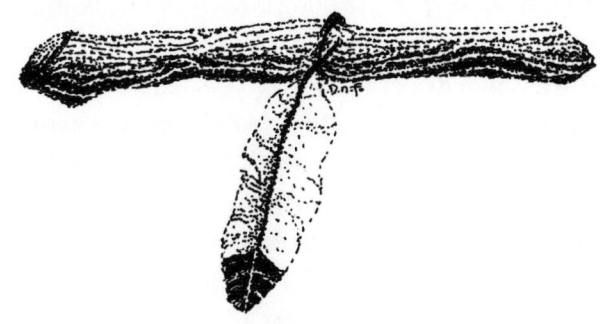

Alana and I sat side-by-side near the cliffs at the far end of the meadow. In front of us was her drum, which she beat slowly and rhythmically. The sound was hypnotic and I was entranced by it, and blissful. It seemed to be saying that the medicine woman was here and that the earth and its creatures were to be healed by her presence.

She paused in her drumming and the meadow fell into silence. Then she resumed the rhythm again, one strong and one soft beat—BOOM. Boom....BOOM. Boom. Gradually, the meadow teemed with slow motion life. The horses appeared, and with them came the deer and the rabbits and other small, furry creatures. They seemed to intermingle, unafraid of each other, moving closer and closer to where we sat.

Alana put the drum mallet on the ground and watched. A rabbit came near to touch the bottom of her moccasin and then it sniffed my shoe, pausing to look at us before it hopped away. Another rabbit came to sniff and touch us on the feet and legs and then another and, with them, came field mice and moles, who did the same thing. As though they waited for the smaller animals to say "hello" first, the horses and deer slowly grazed up to us.

The larger animals, deer and horses, gently nibbled at the grasses around our bodies. A young buck rubbed his antlers against my shoulder. I eased my other hand to his nose, let him sniff it and then I gently touched his face. The coarseness of his fur was a surprise to me and I continued to stroke him in an examining way. A small bird fluttered about the deer's head, watching.

I hesitated to glance at Alana. She was smiling radiantly at me when the buck quietly stepped in front of me to bring his nose next to mine and look me in the eye. His pungent wild smell enveloped me and I sensed that my smell was filling him as well, that our sensitivities were meeting to explore our similarities and our differences. Very gently, I reached up and stroked his neck, then I reached higher to touch the fuzz covering his antlers. He, in turn, licked the side of my face, sniffed my ears, my nose and my mouth. When we had finished, he walked away and continued to graze.

Stony raised his great mustang head and looked across the meadow. I looked in the direction he was looking, noting that Alana was doing the same. Not seeing anything, Stony, Alana and myself looked away again.

There was a rustle in the grasses nearby.

"Ssst...ssst." Alana's lips were separated and she was making the sound through her teeth. "Ssst....ssst," she said again, outstretching her hand.

The grass parted in front of her as a five-foot green snake appeared at her fingertips. Its narrow head rhythmically bobbed up and down and then slid back and forth, sideways, as its tongue darted in and out. Through its movements, the snake seemed to be in communication with Alana. Alana studied the creature and stroked its tiny head with her fingertip, which seemed to calm it. When it had relaxed at her side, I touched it and ran my finger down the length of its body. It stretched to look at me and then it slithered off.

An excited twittering noise escaped from Stony's nostrils and he quickly lifted his head. There, at the far end of the meadow was a black bear who stood on his hind legs, looking in our direction. Stony snorted again and all the animals in the meadow seemed to pay attention. I glanced anxiously at Alana, who seemed calm and undisturbed.

Alana slowly rose to her feet. I rose as well and went with her as she walked away from the animals, out across the meadow toward the bear. She stopped when we were almost upon it. "You must not be afraid, Winged Wolf," she said softly. "Like the other animals, the bear is merely answering the drum's call."

We were not fifty feet from the bear. I thought to comment that the other animals were afraid and that so was I, when the bear dropped to all fours and let out a grunting sound. Alana squatted as well and I was quick to respond. She then imitated the guttural sound like that made by the bear before she rose to her full height again. I managed to stay in unison with her antics.

The bear grunted again and Alana grunted back. The sway of our bodies mimicked the bear's movements and I began to sense that a communication was taking place.

"Do you know what the bear is saying, Winged Wolf?"

I shook my head and muttered that I had no idea.

"He is saying that one of his family is in need of assistance," Alana said, facing me.

Looking at the bear, I shuddered.

"Are you afraid?"

I turned to Alana again. Gazing at her, my uneasiness melted away and I shook my head. "No," I answered, "I am ready to go with you."

Alana took my hand and then released it. "Get behind me, Winged Wolf, and stay there. Stay no more than a foot behind me."

I got directly behind Alana and, when she began to walk toward the bear, I made sure that the foot she raised was the one I raised and that I copied the rhythm of her walk, her every motion and movement. I could see with my peripheral vision to the left and the right of Alana's head, but Alana was my eyes to see directly ahead. Occasionally, I got a glimpse of the bear leading us. After awhile, I became accustomed to the subtleties of Alana's rhythm and moved easily in it.

She stopped and motioned me not to move. Alana leaned down. In front of her was a large, black she-bear, lying on her back. Her front and rear legs were tangled in a maze of wire and nylon net. As Alana looked over it, the bear ceased to struggle. The he-bear who had brought us sat at her side.

"Do you have a knife, Winged Wolf?"

"No," I answered, astounded by the sight. I had some difficulty believing what I was seeing. The bears were sensitive to each other's feelings, the he-bear trying to comfort his mate.

"Go back to my cave, Winged Wolf," Alana said authoritatively, "and get the knife from the ledge near the fireplace. In my herbal mixtures, you will find a jar of yellow salve. Bring it as well."

I was about to hurry off when Alana said, "You must not run. Instead, walk swiftly and carefully."

I left her there, walking as fast as I could to the cave where I gathered up the knife and the salve as she had instructed and hurried to return.

On the way back to meet her, I noticed a large animal on the trail. At first I thought it to be a deer and continued on but, as I approached, I became aware that, while this animal was deer-like in color, it had a powerful hind quarters and a long tail. It was some moments before I allowed myself to recognize that a mountain lion was blocking me.

I fought an impulse to run. Alana had instructed me not to, and I also knew that a lion was one animal who enjoyed a chase. I considered going back to the safety of Alana's cave, but I knew that she needed the items I was carrying to her. There was nothing else for me to do but to continue on.

Mustering all of my courage, I began to walk slowly toward the mountain lion. As I neared, I was so frightened that I could barely breathe and my heart pounded so strongly that I felt sure the lion could hear it. Then, when I was about ten feet away, the huge mountain feline stepped into the bushes on the side of the path to let me pass. I found Alana a short time later. She had already freed one of the she-bear's legs. I handed her the knife.

Alana took the knife and made several cuts in the netting and then she carefully unwound the wire that was still clinging to the bear's other feet. When she had finished, she asked for the salve.

I handed her the jar.

She opened it and dug her fingers into the thick yellow salve, working it into areas where the netting and wire had been. It was then I could see the bruised and torn flesh from the bear's struggle to free herself. When she had finished, the she-bear scrambled to her feet and nuzzled her mate, then the two of them ambled away from us.

Alana turned to me and smiled. "You did well, Winged Wolf," she said.

I smiled appreciatively and told Alana about the mountain lion. I also told her how frightened I had been.

Alana put her arm about my shoulder and gave me a squeeze, then she moved away from me again. "Next time you will not be so frightened," she said. "Your fear is mainly a sign of your lack of experience with companion energy. When you become accustomed to matching energies with all life, you will no longer fear anything." She paused. A hawk swooped down and hovered over us. She pointed to it. "That hawk for instance wants us to know that it has seen us help the bear."

The idea of the hawk watching us was no surprise after all the animal experiences I had had, but I knew that if I hadn't met Alana and spent time with her on the ranch, I would never have believed that a bird had such awarenesses.

"Do you know how it is telling us what it has seen?" Alana asked.

I thought about the hawk and the manner in which it hovered over us.

"When a bird hovers over someone or something, it is watching it," Alana began. "When it hovers and flutters its wings, it is getting your attention to tell you something."

"How do you know what it wants to tell you?" I asked.

"Your own awarenesses will tell you that," Alana answered.

I asked her to explain.

"A medicine woman is like a warrioress, always on the alert. We must be aware of our every action and every reaction," Alana said. "In this way we are tuned to the synchronicity of all life. If a bird flutters around you, it is acknowledging the energy it feels from you. You have to know the energy you are generating." She paused, and anticipated my next question. "And you have to also know the nature of the observer. In this case, you have to know the nature of the bird fluttering around you. As you know, the nature of one species of bird can be quite different from another."

"You mean that a hawk has a different basic nature from a sparrow," I reiterated.

"Exactly. And when you know the energy of the observer and the observed, you come to understand what the hawk is saying. It's as simple as two plus one equals three. Got it?"

"I think so," I said, considering the implications of what she explained. It seemed that, once one understood the individuality of living things, there was an added dimension, a wholeness to life.

Alana began to walk at a quicker pace, which jolted me from my thoughts. I hurried to catch up with her. "Don't think so much about it, Winged Wolf," Alana said, giving me a sideways glance.

"Okay," I answered, trotting alongside her. It was getting late in the day. I felt hungry and realized that it had been many hours since we had eaten.

The luscious aroma of herbs and vegetables stewing over a mesquite fire greeted us as we entered Alana's cave. Terra Lenda was in the kitchen area, fussing over the cooking pot. Bull was seated on the ledge next to her. We said our "hellos" and then Alana went outside to wash at the spring while I took a seat next to Bull and removed my shoe. A small pebble that had been bothering me dropped to the floor.

"I had a stone in my shoe this morning," Bull said.

"Not very comfortable, is it?" I added.

Bull shook his head and sat looking at me as though something was on his mind.

"Anything new down at the house?" I asked.

He shook his head again.

I noticed that while Terra Lenda had her back to us she appeared to be listening. "How was your day, Terra?" I asked.

"Oh, I had a lovely day," she answered, not turning around. Every once in a while, she stirred the stew with a wooden spoon she was holding. "I did a lot of flying today and I saw a great many wonderful things."

I recalled the hawk, wondering if Terra Lenda had occupied its body.

Alana came back into the cave. She went over to Bull and gently stroked the hair on the top of his head and then stepped back to gaze at him. "What's troubling you?" she asked.

Bull shook his head and looked away.

Alana took his chin in her hand and tilted his face to hers. Tears filled Bull's eyes.

"I guess I'd rather be up here with you than down in the house all by myself," Bull said, looking like a hurt puppy. "It's not the same as when Farley was alive."

Alana's expression was compassionate. She let go of his chin. "I know," she said. "I also hoped you learned something from your loneliness."

"What do you mean?" Bull asked.

"Your loneliness is the after-feeling of your anger," Alana said. "You were so strong in your hostility to Heather that you isolated yourself from the joy of others around you."

"But Farley should have left the ranch to me," Bull whined. "I had to have it."

"And you have it, which is good," Alana said, "but the manner in which you got it, was not good."

I wanted to say to both Alana and Bull that I was not unhappy about the outcome, but I knew better than to interfere. Instead I put my shoe back on my foot and slowly tied the laces.

Terra Lenda attended the stew.

"When one fills himself with such strong negative emotions and those emotions effect change in the environment, the outcome is never joyful," Alana added.

"What can I do to make things happy again?" Bull asked childishly.

"Do something for Heather," Alana suggested. "Since you were so angry at her, if you can give her joy, you will become joyful."

As I looked up from tying my shoe, my eyes met Bull's. I smiled at him and said, "I am very happy that I have given you what was rightfully yours."

Bull looked at Alana. "Heather's happy, so it's all right," he said.

Alana shook her head. "No, Bull, it is not all right. You have to make it right with Heather."

"But she said she's glad she gave me the ranch," Bull said.

"It was your anger that convinced her," Alana said. "You must do something special for Heather to make up for it."

Bull turned to me. "What do you want me to do?"

I looked from Bull to Alana, who was not going to suggest anything, and back to Bull again. "Let me think about it," I said.

Bull glanced at Alana who nodded that that was okay. Terra Lenda then handed out bowls of vegetable stew to each of us and the cave fell into silence as we ate hungrily. After my first bowl I told her how delicious it was and then took another half-portion.

Terra glanced up at us with pleasure as we ate. After awhile, she said, "There's a small ranch on the other side of the mountain that went up for sale today."

We all paused to look at her. Since Terra had her own way of coming and going, there was no use asking how she knew.

"Did you know the people who own it?" I asked.

Terra shook her head. "They never spend much time here. California people. I guess they figure it is time to sell." She looked at Alana with a flicker in her eye and grinned. "The house is cute," Terra went on. "It looks to be in good condition too."

"How much do they want for it?" Alana asked.

Terra shrugged her shoulders. "Don't know, but it wouldn't be much. Maybe Heather could buy it and live there." She looked at me and back at Alana again. Then both medicine women looked at me.

I stopped eating and looked back at them. The idea of living on the ranch had appealed to me from the moment I learned of my inheritance. When I signed it over to Bull I had to give up the idea. Now here it was coming back to me again. "It's possible," I said. "I'd like to find out more about it."

Alana studied me. After a moment, she agreed we would go over there the following day.

CHAPTER 11
LIVING AS A
SPIRITUAL WARRIOR

Tommy, the real estate agent from Davis and Harris, was waiting for us in front of a salmon colored, wood frame home, when we pulled up in the Jeep the next afternoon. Alana was sitting in the passenger seat next to me and Bull and Terra were seated in the back. We must have looked a sight because Tommy's jaw dropped when he saw us and his expression was that he didn't believe his eyes—a city girl accompanied by an Indian woman in coveralls, a middle-aged hippie in a buckskin dress and a stocky, little man with a head of hair that stuck out in every direction. I got out of the Jeep first and introduced myself and then the others. I explained that I was the one interested in purchasing the property.

Tommy took us on a tour of the place. There was a small house, a barn big enough for three horses, a two-car garage, three out-buildings and seventy acres of fenced pasture. I was particularly impressed by the tidiness of the place and the fact that the acreage was fenced. It was a perfect home for Spirit, the horse Alana had given me, as well as a few more horses. I liked the place and I could tell that Alana, Terra Lenda and Bull liked it too. I told Tommy that I would think about it and be in touch, then we returned to Farley's Ranch.

No one spoke until we pulled up in front.

"Too bad the house isn't stone, like this one," I said, bringing the Jeep to a stop.

There was a long silence and then Alana asked, "Is that a wish?"

"What do you mean?" I asked.

"Do you wish that house to be stone?"

"I like it as it is, Alana. It's just that I'd like it even better if it was made of stone."

Alana looked at Bull. "Bull helped Farley build this house," Alana said. "He did a good job, don't you think?"

"I sure do," I said.

Bull beamed with pride. "I'm real good at it," he said. Then, as if he had an idea, he added, "If you wanted me to build up stone around your house, I could do it for you. There's plenty of stone out there on the ground."

"You mean you would stone in the house we just looked at?" I asked just to be sure I understood him.

Bull nodded. He looked at Alana for approval and then back to me again.

I realized that Bull had found the gift he would give me in exchange for Farley's Ranch. "You know, I really like that place," I said. "It's a nice size and it has character. The extra out-buildings could be turned into winter houses for Alana and Terra Lenda and maybe, in time, all the buildings can be redone in stone."

Alana and Terra Lenda appeared delighted, which made Bull happy as well. And so it was agreed that I would purchase the place on the other side of the mountain.

Alana and I were seated on the porch steps, watching the sun go down, when she asked me what I felt was the most important thing I had learned from our relationship.

I thought about it a long while before answering. "I think it's that you have refined my ability to live in the now," I said finally. I turned to face her. "Thank you."

"I know I taught you that gratitude is important," Alana said, "but I wish you wouldn't thank me."

"Why?"

"Because every time you thank me, you turn around and blame me for something."

I hesitated, struck by her words. It was true that many times in my apprenticeship, I voiced thanks to Alana and then turned around and mentally whipped her for the very thing for which I had expressed gratitude. We were talking about the twin aspects of praise and blame, flip sides of a coin and, while I was always disturbed and ashamed of myself for going to the opposite side, I knew that it was still something that I occasionally did. I also knew that Alana was aware of my thoughts, whether I spoke them aloud or not. "How can I stop it from happening?" I finally asked.

"For the time being, why don't you keep your *thank yous* to yourself," Alana said. "That way you'll be filled with unspoken thoughts of gratitude and there won't be any room for blame."

We sat quietly awhile. I thought about praise and blame and my work in the world, and I knew that the praise that some people heaped on me for my work with Alana gave rise to criticism from others. It seemed that opposite feelings were at work no matter what one did or did not do. I told Alana about my realization.

"Opposites are always at work—in action, as well as thought," Alana added.

"I don't understand," I said.

"When something moves, something follows."

"Huh?"

"When you move away from something, it follows you," Alana explained. "I call a horse to me by backing up. It works the same way with people and the situations they act out."

I recalled how Alana took a few steps backwards when she was summoning a horse to her, which I understood as horse language to "come up," but I didn't see how it related to people and situations. I asked her to explain what she meant.

Alana hesitated, looking out to the horizon and then suddenly stood up and began to walk away. I jumped to my feet and hurried after her. Suddenly, she stopped again and turned to face me. "Do you see what I mean?" she asked.

I stood dumbfounded, aware that Alana had demonstrated the principle we were discussing by walking away from me. In turn, I was following her.

"Now go back to those porch steps and sit down," Alana instructed.

Reluctantly, I returned to the porch steps and sat down. Alana remained standing a short distance away. A moment later, she turned and began walking toward the mountains. I checked myself, fighting an impulse to follow her. As I watched her disappear into the shadow of the mountainside, I realized another dimension to the principle she had demonstrated—that, while my body had remained seated on the porch, my attention, soul, had followed her and remained with her.

I spent the night at the house with Bull. Early the next morning

I set out to find Alana. She was outside her cave, petting a lizard when I found her.

"Good morning, Alana," I called.

"Did you sleep well in that comfortable bed?" Alana asked, putting the lizard down on a rock next to the cave entrance to give her attention to me. Instead of scurrying off, it stretched itself on its little legs and looked at us.

"I sure did," I said, aware that I remembered nothing after my head touched the pillow. I must have gone straight to sleep.

"You will be leaving soon, Winged Wolf."

I shouldn't have been surprised, but I was. "When?"

"Not for awhile yet, but soon," Alana said. "I don't want you to lose your momentum in the world."

It was true that I had totally forgotten my life back in California and that I didn't care if I ever wrote another book or gave another lecture. I was so happy on the ranch with Alana that I couldn't bear the thought of leaving.

"There are some matters that I want to clear up with you," Alana said. "Did you bring your protection stick?"

"It's in your cave," I answered.

"Go and get it and then we will talk."

I went inside Alana's cave, to the ledge in the kitchen area where I had left my stick and went back outside. Alana was walking across the field to a circle of boulders. She sat down on one of them as I hurried to join her. The horses were grazing in the distance, moving closer with each mouthful. As soon as I sat down, Alana began to speak.

"The difference between a spiritual warrior and an ordinary person is that when an ordinary person gets their hands tied behind their back, they are rendered helpless. When a warrior's hands are tied behind her back, she is just as helpless but her helplessness is constructive and purposeful, a path walk." Alana paused to study me. "Do you know what I am telling you, Winged Wolf?"

"I think so," I answered. "You are saying that a spiritual warrior makes lemonade out of lemons."

"Something very much like that," Alana said. "Since a warrior knows the laws and principles of life, she can live freely without her viewpoint trapping her. She is constantly moving ahead even if she is sitting still with her hands tied behind her back."

"You mean a spiritual warrior uses every opportunity to learn," I rephrased. "For instance, if I had my hands tied behind my back my calmness could control my fear and discomfort."

"Exactly," Alana said, nodding in agreement. "But there are also other alternatives." She looked deeply into my eyes and I sensed that she was looking directly into the core of me. "You will find that every little seed I plant in you can produce a fruit that has a thousand uses," Alana went on. "Nothing I have taught you means only one thing. Each lesson benefits every aspect of your life, as well as the whole. Do you understand, Winged Wolf?"

I answered that I did and that I was grateful for what I had learned from her, and then I fell silent again.

"Someone who wants to be a Shaman is either confused, or in extreme pain, or devoted to spiritual growth," Alana continued. "Extreme pain can mean that they are very unhappy and their circumstances force them to seek a greater meaning to life. These are the people who will mostly come to you and ask to be your students. Beware. These people will want miracles from you to change their lives. When they are feeling good, they will praise you, and when they are feeling bad, they will blame you."

I lowered my head, ashamed for the many times I believed Alana to have mistreated me and how I had blamed her for my unhappiness.

Alana took my chin in her hand and raised my head. "No, Winged Wolf, it is not the same with you. You are a spiritual warrior, dedicated to spiritual growth. Your intent with me has been pure. It is a person's intent that you must come to recognize." She let go of my chin and continued to look deeply into me. "If you are not sure of a person's intent, then take the time to decide if you can help them fix their lives or if they wish you to change things for the better. Herein, lies the clue as to whether you can work with someone or not. A shaman fixes things, rather than changes things. Fixing things in a person means filling their holes or working on that part of a person that is not alive, working on the part that has no spirit. It is a difficult job because the person you are helping will think that you are often being cruel in your treatment of them. And they will fight you, even hate you sometimes. You, in turn, will love them, because you are giving so much of yourself to help them fix themselves. It will, at times, be very painful for you."

I sat quietly, remembering how I had felt and acted toward Alana when she had been firm with me. Finally, I said, "I know I have been a difficult student, that I argued with you and resisted what you tried to teach me. It strikes me as odd that I craved that which I resisted. I still do."

Alana smiled. "There is no doubt that you are a challenge," she said, "but remember this: If you poke someone and there is no response, you can't put something into them." She paused and then added, "A teacher pokes a student until that student lets go of their personal history, meaning they eliminate their rigid attitudes and aberrations. It is not an easy job, Winged Wolf, but a rewarding one." She smiled radiantly at me.

I remembered a time when I was depressed and Alana snapped at me and told me to lighten up, that I was draining her energy. She then told me to smile, to show the light in my eyes. I had forced a smile, making my eyes fill with the light of anger. She had smiled at me then and said, "That's better." I reminded her of the incident and asked her why she had preferred my anger to my depression.

Alana's expression sobered again. "You were depressed, Winged Wolf, and depression is merely another form of anger, anger turned inward. It was draining to the both of us. When I forced you to smile, you re-routed your anger into your smile, which vitalized you and quit draining me."

I was astounded by her clarity.

Alana burst out laughing. "When I met you, you were always looking in at yourself," she continued. "I had to turn you around and get you to look out. The mind quiets when we look out and then we are able to move away from our aberrations. When you are not looking at yourself, you cannot be guilty of judging others. Love is looking out at the world—looking out means viewpoint of Soul. When you are cheerful, you are looking out at the world. When you are sad, you are looking at yourself."

I took some minutes to think about what she had said and then asked, "What are the things I must do to become a shaman?"

Alana looked at me for a very long time before answering. Her deep-blue eyes were like a vortex of energy and I was being drawn into them, into her. I was filled with bliss. "The three steps to becoming a shaman are 1) the ability to fast, 2) the practice of silence, and 3) contemplation on the teachings I give you. In this way, there is nothing you will not know, nor nothing you cannot do." Alana paused and then explained, "Shamans can fall between the wind on many subjects that they are not kin with. When you go to help someone, because your intent will be to help fix what needs mending in a person's life, you will find that you often fall into a knowledge belt that is not your own. For instance, I once worked with a young sculptor and he and I spent many hours sculpting together. And you, Winged Wolf, have made me a poet." She smiled again, then turned her head and raised a hand to pat Stony on the shoulder.

I had been so engrossed that I hadn't paid attention to the horses, nor how close they had come to us.

"There are some basic rules I would have you remember, Winged Wolf," Alana said, looking from Stony to me.

I gave her my complete attention.

"When you are put in a difficult situation, remember that every time a chicken shakes, another chicken is there to peck at him."

I laughed and said that I understood, that I would not let fear stand in the way of what I wanted to do.

"Pay no attention to another person's display of ego," Alana then said. "Big egos have to live up to their stories. Always put these people to work. If they give you a problem, get them in a threatening situation and keep them there. They will have no time to be a difficulty for you. Remember, you make energy by shifting the existing energy." She paused and then said, "There is something else that I want you to be aware of. Most people illuminate the part of themselves they want you to see. They shine a light on the illumination that already exists in them, rather than trying to illuminate the dark side of themselves. It's the way much of today's mentality works and it's not healthy."

I was aware that Alana was telling me all these things now, out of context of the things we were doing, as though she was rushing to give me some bits and pieces before I left. The realization saddened me.

Suddenly, Alana rose to her feet, patted Stony, and turned to me. "Winged Wolf, do you remember the large crystal we once saw at Swede's Feed Store?"

"Yes," I answered, saying that I remembered it well, that I had often thought about and wished that I had purchased it.

"Good," Alana said, "because I want you to go into town now and buy it and return to me with it."

I started to say that we had seen it a long time ago and that it may have been sold, but another part of me knew that it was waiting for me. I looked up to the sun, which was now overhead. "I should be back by mid-afternoon," I said.

Alana nodded and replied that she would stay in the area and wait for me until I returned.

I walked off and had gone quite a distance when I heard Alana calling to me. I quickly turned around.

Alana was facing the horses with one arm extended in front of her, directing the horses to singly jump over an invisible hurdle. I was awed and astounded by the sight. Each horse approached a specific area and then leapt at least four feet as though to rise above an obstacle and then trotted away. It was the most amazing thing I had seen Alana do. I watched as the horses leapt higher and higher to scale the hurdle that wasn't there. Alana finally brought the activity to a halt and disbanded the horses. She stood looking in my direction for a long time and waved me to go on my way.

When I had gotten to the feed store I told Swede that I wanted to purchase the crystal I had seen with Alana.

"That sure is funny," he said. "My wife was just cleanin it up today." He went behind the counter and pointed to it in the display case. "It's a beauty, isn't it?"

"It sure is," I answered. "How much do you want for it?"

"Well, my wife's decided she likes havin it around. If I let it go too cheap, she'd skin me."

"How much do you think she'd want for it?" I asked.

He hesitated. "Bout a hundred and fifty dollars. It's a lot of money, but this here crystal has got no broken points on it and it's one of the biggest I've seen." He carefully took it out of the display case and put it on top of the counter. It was perfect and beautiful.

"All right, I'll take it," I said and, reaching in my pocket, I withdrew the money and gave it to him. "Do you have some paper I can wrap around it to protect it?" I asked.

"Sure!" Swede went into the back room and returned with a piece of white butcher paper. He wrapped it carefully and handed it to me. "How's Alana?" he asked.

"She's fine," I told him.

"The crystal for her?"

I shook my head. "It's for me, Swede. I remembered seeing it a year ago and I often wished that I had bought it."

He nodded that he understood. "Well now ya did," he said. "Enjoy it."

I thanked him and started out the door.

"Heather!" he called.

I turned around.

"Tell Alana I've been eatin lots of cherries like she told me but I still got the gout."

"I'll tell her," I said and left the store.

When I got back to the ranch, I hurried to find Alana. She was in the meadow near her cave, grooming the horses.

I tore the paper away from around the crystal and unwrapped it. Immediately the sunlight touched it and made it look like it was on fire.

Alana smiled approvingly as she looked at it, then asked how Swede was feeling.

I told her what he said.

"Eating cherries cures gout only if you are careful with the rest of your diet," she said. "I told him not to eat any meat, dairy products or other rich foods." She took the crystal from my hands and moved it about in the sunlight. The effect was dazzling. After a moment, she turned to me. "I want you to stay up here with your crystal for the next few days. It would be best if you carry it with you everywhere you go because I want you to spend as much time as you can, studying it. Memorize every point on it and how it stands in relation to the other points, how the points have grown out of the base of the crystal. I want you to familiarize yourself with this crystal so completely that you will never forget what it looks like." She looked up at me. "Okay?"

"Okay," I answered.

She handed me the crystal and told me to find a comfortable spot to sit and study it.

CHAPTER 12

FLIGHT OF WINGED WOLF

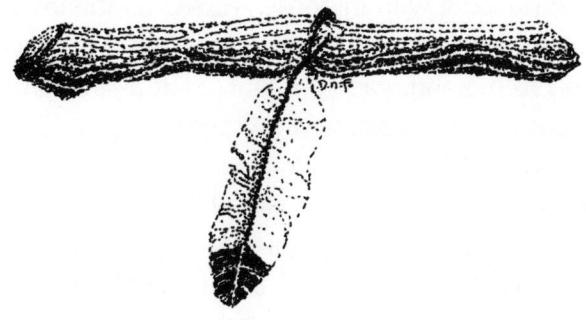

Alana left me for a few days to familiarize myself with the crystal. At her instructions, every morning I would get up, straighten my bed at the back of the cave and take out my crystal. I came to recognize its detail, silhouetted in semi-darkness as well as full light. In the brilliance of the day, I found such miracles embedded in it as rainbows, crystalline forests, specks of gold and crimson. Also, I came to see how the crystal columns grew out of a mass of dense fissure, and I noticed that the most transparent part of the base was where the crystal columns had grown the largest, and that, where there were no columns, the light did not pass through. Most of all, I realized that the crystal was a living thing, that in eons of geologic time it had grown to be what it was and that it was still growing.

On occasion I would rise to my feet and stand over it, studying how it blended with the green from the meadow. It seemed natural for it to rest in the meadow grasses, a glowing vortex of color and light, adapting to the environment.

Gradually, I came to know the crystal so well that I developed a sense of what it would be like to be inside it, looking out at the world from its center. Sometimes my imagination played that I was inside the crystal, walking through it, climbing from one level to another, or standing with my nose pressed on the inside of one crystal column, looking into another. The crystal world became a companion to me and, gazing into it, I felt as though I was an explorer, energized by each new discovery.

On the afternoon of the fourth day, I was lying on my back in the sunny meadow with my eyes closed, the crystal resting on my abdomen, when I suddenly thought of Alana. I wondered if I could imagine her into the crystal as well, and if I could conjure the same sense of reality with her in it together with me. Thoughtfully, I opened my eyes to gaze into the sky. Alana was standing over me.

I was surprised and sat up, aware that she held a cloth bag in her hand. "Hello, Alana," I said, not totally certain if she was there or not.

Alana sat down next to me and looked at my crystal, and asked what I had learned about it.

I told her all that I had observed and then added the fantasies that I had felt about being inside of the crystal, as well as looking out from inside it; and how I was about to envision her into the scene when I opened my eyes and there she was.

Alana listened until I was finished. She then reached inside of the cloth bag and took out a napkin and on it she put some bread and cheese. She broke the bread and cut a slice of cheese, handing me some of each. "Today will be the most important day of your life, Winged Wolf," she said, glancing at me and then at the food we were about to eat.

I kept quiet.

"Eat," she said, "but eat slowly. I don't want you rushing anything this day."

The overhead sun warmed the top of my head and slowly passed behind a cloud. When it reappeared, I bit into my bread and cheese and chewed slowly, savoring it as Alana had instructed. If I would have said anything to her, I would have said how happy I was; that I felt fulfilled and free and ready for anything that life could hand out. I knew that what I felt was because of the concentrated attention Alana had given me. She had totally turned me around from the person I was when I first visited the ranch. She had scrubbed me clean in a way that I was becoming the person I wanted to be.

I turned to Alana but she was eating and ignored my look, and so I continued to be silent while I finished the food she had brought me.

A ground squirrel scurried across the field and, as I looked after it, I saw deer and the horses. It struck me that in Alana's absence, I had seen no animals. Now there was life everywhere. I mentioned this to Alana.

"The animals tend to think that I am their mother and so they follow me," Alana answered lightly.

I chuckled. It was obvious that what she said was true by the sudden display of life returning to the hollow.

"Do you have any questions about the crystal?" Alana asked.

"Yes. What is a crystal?"

"A rock."

I stared at her, certain that she had more of an explanation to offer than that.

"What did you want me to say, Winged Wolf?"

"I thought you might tell me about the crystal," I said.

"What would you like to hear?"

"What a crystal is?"

"A rock."

Alana had given me no opening to continue my line of questioning, so I said, "A beautiful rock."

"A beautiful rock," Alana agreed.

I felt dissatisfied but said nothing.

Alana glared at me. "What does it matter?"

"I was just curious."

"About what?"

"About the nature of the crystal."

"You will learn its nature for yourself."

I waited for Alana to tell me how.

"I wanted you to buy that crystal and to memorize it because it is going to be the anchor or a ground for the rest of your life. Actually it is like a grounding cord." Alana paused, studying me.

I thought of a steel pipe that is sunk deeply into the earth to make a ground for a hot wire fence and I asked her if my analogy was correct.

"Yes," Alana answered, and then she continued. "You are going to bury the crystal someplace. Before you die, you will come back to it. It will make it possible for you to leave the earth, especially if you are in a confused state of mind."

"Huh?" I didn't understand her theory that the crystal would make it possible for me to leave the earth, but I was more concerned over the immediate suggestion, that I was going to die.

"Everyone dies," Alana snapped.

"When?"

"When what?"

"When am I going to die?" I asked sadly.

"That's for you to decide," Alana said. "You can live to be an old woman, or you can choose to die today."

"Alana, I don't wish to die today."

"I didn't say you should," Alana snapped. "Why are you so concerned with yourself? If you don't want to die, you won't die. But you will die, someday."

I relaxed and let out a sigh.

"It is a spiritual warrior's job to prepare for her death so that she is not the effect of someone else's preparedness. Do you understand, Winged Wolf?"

"I think so," I said.

"You must decide where you want to bury your crystal," Alana said.

"Can I bury it in California?"

"If you want to."

I hesitated. I didn't really want to bury the crystal in California. I merely wanted to find out the rules. "I'd rather bury it here, in the mountains," I said. "That way I'll come back before I die."

"Do you know where in the mountains?" Alana asked.

The first image that came to mind was the ledge on the side of the cliff where Alana and Terra Lenda had said that they wanted to teach me flying but, since it was inaccessible, I quickly dismissed it. "No," I said finally, then asked if Alana had any ideas.

"I have lots of ideas but they are not yours," she answered. She rose to her feet. "Maybe if we go for a walk, the place will come to you," she said.

I hurried to my feet with the crystal in my hands.

"Do you have your protection stick?" Alana asked.

"I'll get it," I answered, hurrying inside the cave and taking it from over my bed. When I went back outside, Terra Lenda was with Alana.

"Hello, Terra," I said, smiling uneasily. She was holding a long piece of rope in her hand.

Terra grinned at me, then glanced at the crystal and protection stick I held. "Looks like you're ready." Terra then whispered something in Alana's ear.

Alana chuckled. "Tell Heather," she said.

"Bull is collecting stones for your house, Heather," Terra said.

"That's wonderful," I added, smiling. Then it occurred to me that he had no way of transporting them from one side of the mountain to the other and I said so to Alana.

"It doesn't matter," Alana said, looking hard at me. "Why do you insist on picking up on things that don't matter?"

"I don't know," I answered, then added, "habit, I guess."

"Winged Wolf, you cannot bring your habits with you today." Alana paused, then added, "Your habits have the power to destroy you."

I nodded.

"No," Alana said, "nodding that you understand is not good enough. What is it that you understand?"

I hesitated, choosing my words carefully. "My habits are yesterday's clothing," I said. "When I wear them I am unable to live in the freedom I have earned today."

"You have earned nothing until the habits are broken," Alana said harshly. "Habits are formed by living lazily. A person who lives by habit doesn't have to think much. A warrior must think freely and intelligently." She paused, looking hard at me. "You think me a difficult teacher, but if I were to let you go on your merry way, living in habit, I would be no teacher at all."

"Thank you," I said, feeling ashamed.

Alana let out a sigh and turned to Terra Lenda.

"I think she's ready," Terra said sincerely. "That is, once she plants her crystal, she'll be ready."

I looked from Alana to Terra and back to Alana again. Whatever the two medicine women were planning, they were keeping it a secret.

Alana suggested that I put the crystal in the cloth bag in which she had brought lunch and tie it to my waist with the length of rope Terra held.

I carefully placed the crystal deep inside the cloth bag and folded the remainder of the material around it. Alana then held it to the small of my back and Terra secured it with the rope, tying it tightly around my waist.

"Ugh, not so tight, Terra," I pleaded.

"Yes, be careful, you might break a habit for her, Terra," Alana joked.

I gave Alana a look to say that wasn't funny but she burst out laughing. "Don't take yourself so seriously, Winged Wolf. If Terra could break a habit for you, you should be glad." She cracked up laughing again, obviously thinking her joke to be very funny.

Terra Lenda only smiled. She tested the rope around my waist by pulling down on it, which loosened it as well. "Is that better?" she asked.

"Yes, thank you." I glanced at Alana who was sober again.

"Turn around," Alana said.

I turned around with my back to her.

"Now run fifty strides, Winged Wolf."

I began to run, counting to be sure I would run the strides that Alana asked. The crystal stayed tightly and comfortably secured to the small of my back. When I had gone the distance, I stopped. As I turned and waited for Alana and Terra Lenda to catch up I realized my breath was surprisingly normal and that I felt exhilarated.

Alana and Terra finally caught up with me. "Why did you stop?"

Alana appeared annoyed.

"Because you told me to run fifty strides, which I did."

"I was just giving you an idea of how far I wanted you to run," Alana said. "This time don't count. Run ahead and keep running until you feel inclined to stop." She paused. "Note that I used the word inclined, meaning to stop when your intuitive nature wants you to stop. In that stopping place you will decide where you want to bury your crystal."

I nodded that I understood and then started to trot off.

"Winged Wolf, stop!" Alana called.

I stopped and turned around.

"You must sit in the center of your head during this run or else you will become confused."

"Okay," I answered appreciatively, hesitating to be sure Alana had finished speaking.

"Well, go on," she urged.

I trotted away, leaving Alana and Terra behind. I didn't run as fast as before and, this time, I was more observant of the scenery as I passed. Also, while I was accustomed to sitting in the center of my head, or using soft vision, I was particularly sure that I was using my peripheral senses, which assures that the mind is silent, so that my intuition would be free to direct me. On one occasion, however, I thought of my life in California and the work that lay ahead for me, and I thought too, about the ranch on the other side of the mountain and what life would be like if I moved there.

I ran and ran and ran until I could run no more. My feet came to a sudden halt and I bent over, my hands locked on the flesh just above my knees to brace myself as I tried to catch my breath. After some minutes, I stood erect again. Alana and Terra Lenda were watching me. I was surprised to see that they had caught up with me so quickly and that they were not in the least out of breath.

"Your intuition is triggered in a peculiar way," Alana said. She came over and placed her hand on my chest to feel my heartbeat, then she stepped back to look at me. "Why is it that you have to reach the end of your rope before it kicks in?"

I didn't know what she was talking about and so I remained silent.

Alana turned and looked around at the terrain. The cliffs were close and just above us was the ledge where the two medicine women had wanted me to fly. Terra Lenda now stood quietly in the background. I was amazed that I had run so far a distance without stopping to catch my breath. Alana turned to me. "Well, Winged Wolf, where will it be?"

"Where will what be?"

"Where you bury your crystal."

I shook my head. While the ledge had been my first consideration, I knew that it was impossible. The rock getting up to it was smooth and I did not have any rock climbing equipment. "I haven't found the spot yet," I said finally. "I only stopped to catch my breath."

"You stopped because your intuition trapped you," Alana said. "It pushed your body to the end of a long rope to get you to listen to it."

"I don't know what you mean," I said confused. "I haven't chosen to bury my crystal here."

Alana looked at me for a long time. "Winged Wolf, it is not your fault that you do not understand. I never explained intuition to you." She paused and then continued. "Intuition is our inner voice, but that doesn't necessarily mean that it speaks to us in words. Usually the inner voice speaks to us through an urge. We feel a nudge to do something, or we are attracted to something without an explanation why. I would bet that you had an impulse to pick this spot to bury your crystal before your body actually arrived here." She paused, studying me. "Is it true?"

I nodded. "When you first mentioned burying the crystal, I thought of this place," I said, "but I dismissed the idea because it wasn't practical."

Alana dropped her jaw without opening her mouth, which pursed her lips in an "Oh, I see" expression.

"Of course, I realize that intuition isn't necessarily practical," I said, responding to her unspoken reply. "But it seems to me that if it can be practical, all the better." I paused to carefully choose my words. "That's why I decided to go for another place."

"But you haven't gone to another place," Terra piped up, coming up next to Alana. "You're here, Winged Wolf and you exhausted yourself to get here."

"I can go on," I said, feeling refreshed.

The two medicine women looked at one another and then at me. Alana squinted her eyes as she looked at me. "Winged Wolf, you are to continue on your journey. Go and find a place to bury your crystal."

I was relieved and thanked her for her understanding. Then I checked the rope around my waist to be sure the crystal was still securely tied and trotted off.

I hadn't gone far when I realized that I was entering territory that I had never explored. The cliffs were becoming sharper and more jagged and passage between them was closer and more difficult. I stopped, suddenly out of breath, and looked around. I wondered if I was still on Farley's Ranch. Not only was the terrain noticeably different, but there was a feeling to the area that I didn't like. I argued with myself that if I kept going my feeling would change and I would find a spot to bury the crystal but I knew that it wasn't true. Then I argued that I had gone too far, that I should not have gone as far as the ledge where I had left Alana and Terra, but I knew that that wasn't true either. I had had no inclination to stop.

I took a deep breath and spun around. The ledge was where I had thought to bury the crystal in the first place. If Alana was right, and she usually was, I was using practicality as an excuse. In this case, it was a habitual excuse that I made whenever a task seemed tough. I began walking back to where I had left Alana and Terra Lenda.

The two medicine women were waiting for me and saw me immediately as I came into view. As I neared, Terra Lenda smiled but Alana shook her head as if to say that "I was stubborn and a slow learner."

"You were right," I said. "This is the place."

"What brought you to that conclusion?" Alana asked.

"I didn't like it up there," I answered, pointing in the direction from where I had come. "The terrain made me feel uneasy, like I had entered another world."

"It wasn't the terrain that made you uneasy, Winged Wolf," Alana said. She paused to study me. "Your uneasiness was caused by the fact that you had gone too far. You moved so far away from your target that you could no longer see the bull's-eye. In other words, you were out of the element you chose for yourself."

I was struck by Alana's words and hesitated to stare at her. I knew what she said was true and, I also knew that, if I never learned anything else, this one lesson was worth my whole journey.

"Where will you bury your crystal, Winged Wolf?" Alana prompted.

From the tone of her question, it occurred to me that Alana did not know of my attraction for the ledge. I was relieved and quickly decided to change the location. I began to look around on the ground, peeking behind rocks and in crevices, as if trying to locate the perfect spot.

Alana used the time to visit with Terra Lenda. The two medicine women chatted about the weather and the changing of seasons, the smell of autumn in the air, arguing between themselves over when the first snowfall would come. It was irritating to me to have to listen to them in the background and, as I went from one spot to another, I wished that they would be quiet. Finally, I turned around and told them what I felt.

Both Alana and Terra Lenda burst out laughing.

I was insulted. "Why are you laughing at me?"

Alana stopped laughing and glared at me. "Why do you think we're laughing?"

"I'm trying to find a place to bury this crystal," I said annoyed.

"And we're trying to entertain ourselves while you figure things out," Alana said.

I thought of telling her that she could be more respectful to me and my mission, but I kept quiet.

The medicine women began to converse again. This time they talked about my habit of practicality and how it formed notches in my brain.

I suddenly caught on. Alana and Terra were trying to let me know that they were aware of my procrastination. I stopped fumbling and looked at them. Although I didn't know how I'd succeed, I decided that, if they thought I could accomplish getting up to the ledge, then I would make every effort to do so. "Okay," I said and looked up to the ledge above their heads. "I'll bury the crystal up there."

Alana turned to see where I had pointed and then reached out her hand to me. "Take my hand," she said.

I took her hand.

"Now walk with me, and use your soft vision," she instructed.

I clutched my protection stick in my right hand and began to walk with her. As we walked hand-in-hand I noticed that my inner and outer vision was diffused in a soft vision way. Alana led me to the left and then to the right, in circles and squares. For a moment, it seemed as though we were sinking into the earth and then rising again. Instead of stepping over rocks along our path, we seemed to be walking through them. She led me to the face of the cliff and, without hesitation, together we stepped into the rock, where it was deep and dark and yet very much alive. After a moment, we came out into the sunlight again and Alana let go of my hand. She turned me to face the rock. "Run, Winged Wolf, run!"

Without hesitation I ran into the face of the cliff and entered the rock. Again I was swept up in darkness but, gradually, in it, I began to perceive an energy that was similar to light. Electrical impulses darted like lightning in the otherwise total darkness. I watched them, how they took shape and form and how they expanded and contracted. After some time, I came to realize that they were magnifying my impulses. When I thought of moving forward, they expanded and, when I thought of moving backward, they became small and drawn into themselves. I tried speaking but, instead of my voice, I heard a peculiar hum and the electrical impulses danced to its sound. The hum intensified and followed me as I moved deeper and deeper into the rock. Then it stopped. Suddenly I realized that I was in control of the forces around me. My energy— thoughts and feelings—was at the root of that control. There was truly mind over matter, truly a oneness with all life. The crystal, tied to the small of my back, was to be planted on the ledge as a reminder of the importance of the experience I was having. Alana had said that it would serve as my anchor for the rest of my life, to constantly touch me with what I had learned, with what I was learning. I drew in a cool, deep breath and, feeling contentment like

I had never felt before, I stepped out of the rock and back into the sunlight.

The birds flew past me. As I watched them, diving in play, I became aware that I was not on the ground but on the ledge on the side of the cliff. I looked below but Alana and Terra Lenda were not there. Instead I saw a large bird sitting on a rock, and next to it a furry, tan colored animal with a large tail, looking up at me. I wondered where the medicine women had gone and continued to scan the terrain for them but they were nowhere to be seen.

I untied the crystal from around my waist and removed it from the cloth bag. It immediately came alive in the sunlight. Streaks of gold and crimson sparkled from its pinnacles shooting an array of color and patterns on the rock. I carefully set it down next to the soft, sandy soil against the deepest wall, then I picked up a loose shale of rock and dug a hole more than a foot deep. When I had finished, I placed the crystal into the hole and covered it. As I patted the soil firmly in place, I thought of what Alana had said about the buried crystal acting as my ground, saying that the crystal worked in the same way that a metal stake serves to ground a hot wire fence. The metal stake freed the electricity to enter the wire. When I died, the crystal would make it possible for me to leave the earth. I still didn't understand the ceremony and I didn't really care. I only knew that I was learning to be a student and that my life was moving positively forward. With gratitude in my heart, I turned and looked around. The cliff was smooth. There were no crevices to hold my hands and feet. The rope that had tied the crystal around my waist was far too short to be of any use. How would I get down?

I sat down to think and, as I did, a hawk flew past me and then returned, fluttering its wings to hover in front of me. I quickly looked below again. The large bird that had been on the rock was gone, but the furry animal was still there.

The hawk screeched to regain my attention and then I knew. Terra Lenda had come to remind me that I was an eagle. As though I had been struck a blow, I looked down to the furry animal again and this time I knew. It was a badger that looked back at me. It was Alana.

As though in agreement, the hawk screeched again and then flew away.

I breathed deeply and slowly and finally closed my eyes. It was as though I heard Alana call up to me, "Fly, Winged Wolf—fly!"

**Other books
by Heather Hughes-Calero**

Woman Between the Wind

Writing as a Tool for Self-Discovery

The Golden Dream

The Sedona Trilogy
  Book 1: Through the Crystal
  Book 2: Doorway Between the Worlds
  Book 3: Land of Nome

HEATHER HUGHES-CALERO is the author of more than a hundred national magazine articles and seven metaphysical books, including **Writing As a Tool for Self-Discovery,** which was a recently featured selection of the Writer's Digest Book Club. Following the success of **The Sedona Trilogy** and **The Golden Dream,** Heather began teaching writing as a vehicle for personal liberation, conducting special workshops throughout the United States and taught adult education classes at Monterey Peninsula College. Her books, **Woman Between the Wind** and **The Flight of Winged Wolf,** are an exciting firsthand account of her adventure and training with a Sioux medicine woman.

Hughes-Calero's interest in anthropology and dedication to living life through experience caused her to spend years researching religion and different cultures. During one of her many quests, she worked in Japan with translators, translating the "heart" discourse of the Lotus Sutra from Sanskrit to English. Through her life study as a writer and student of spiritual growth, she discovered a doorway to the creative imagination and higher consciousness that lives in all of us. Her seminars, books and tapes provide a multidimensional exploration in the search for self through the release of creative expression.